UNDERSTANDING

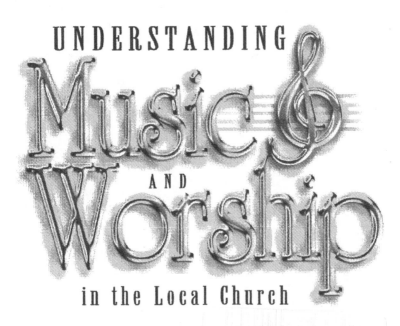

Music & AND Worship

in the Local Church

D0961697

by
Vernon M. Whaley, Ph.D.

Evangelical Training Association

110 Bridge Street • Box 327

Wheaton, IL 60189-0327

Scripture quotations are from the New American Standard Bible, © The Lockman Foundation 1960, 1962, 1963, 1971, 1972, 1973, 1975, and is used by permission.

2002 Edition

ISBN: 0-910566-65-8

Contents

Man was made to worship God. God gave to man a harp and said, "Here above all the creatures I have made and created I have given you the largest harp. I put more strings on your instrument and I have given you a wider range than I have given to any other creature. You can worship me in a manner that no other creature can." And when he sinned man took that instrument and threw it down in the mud and there it has lain for centuries, rusty, broken, unstrung; and man, instead of playing a harp like the angels and seeking to worship God in all of his activities, is egocentered and turns in on himself and sulks, and swears, and laughs, and sings, but it's all without joy and without worship.

– A. W. Tozer from
Worship: The Missing Jewel
in the Evangelical Church

Why Study
Music & Worship?

1

There the woman stood, stunned by what she thought was the sheer arrogance of a man who seemed to know her every thought. "Our fathers worshiped in this mountain," she declared, "and you people say that Jerusalem is the place where men ought to worship." Having just been confronted with her very own sinfulness, she wanted to argue about the mode and place of worship. She was asking Jesus, "O.K. Mr. Know–it–all Prophet—where are we supposed to worship?"

Worship, and the music that is an integral part of it, can be pretty confusing at times. So why study music and worship? We should study these subjects, as A. W. Tozer wrote, because we are "made to worship God." Every picture we have of heaven reveals angelic beings worshiping God (Isa. 6:1–6). John's vision of heaven unveils the majestic sight of those from every tribe, tongue, people, and nation, gathered around the throne of God—worshiping (Rev. 5:9–10). When Jesus triumphantly entered Jerusalem, the Pharisees asked Him to rebuke His disciples who were worshiping Him. Instead, Jesus rebuked the Pharisees, "I tell you, if these become silent, the stones will cry out!" (Luke 19:37–40). The study of worship is important because it is what believers will be doing for eternity!

Many people view music and worship like the Samaritan woman Jesus encountered in John 4. She had heard all the arguments for years whether Samaria or Jerusalem was the correct place to worship God. It was easier for her to argue about worship than to acknowledge her need for worship. Evangelicals face a similar situation today. Take worship styles among evangelical churches, for example. There are probably as many different styles of worship as there are churches. This leads to two important questions. What approach to worship is the *best* one? What is a *biblical* approach to music and worship?

To stimulate your thinking, consider the following hypothetical interviews of ministers of music and worship at five very different churches. Keep in mind, these are not real churches. Rather, these are composite sketches of what I have found in real churches I have visited, from various denominations and locations, during my years of ministry. Chances are you have visited some of these churches as

5

well, or ones like them. It is even possible you are a member of a church like one of these five.

In these interviews, each hypothetical music and worship minister was asked, "Would you tell me about the practice of music and worship at your church and what you believe is the key to your approach?"

Anything Is O.K. With Us Church

We take a pretty laid back approach to music and worship here at the O.K. Church. Basically, whatever kind of music you like is O.K. We take seriously what Paul wrote in 1 Corinthians 14:26, "each one has a psalm." If someone wants to come on up and join the choir during the service, it's O.K. with us. We are always looking for people who can play instruments or sing solos. You can never have too many people involved or spend enough time praising the Lord!

We ask—is this music speaking to somebody's heart? You never know who will be in our services. We might have someone who loves country music, or who enjoys the blues, or likes traditional hymns. I can tell you this, if he stays around here long enough, he will hear exactly the kind of music that speaks to his heart.

You can probably tell we have a lot of congregational participation in our worship services. That's the way we've planned it. We want our people to be able to share what's in their hearts. And that's O.K. with us!

The First Church of Current Styles & Trends

Music and worship are very important to us here at First Current. The primary thing that drives us is the desire be on the cutting edge for the Lord. For us, that means we use only the most current songs. As David wrote in Psalm 33:3: "Sing to Him a new song; play skillfully with a shout of joy." We try to do both in all our worship services.

If the Christian publishers come out with something new, we want it—yesterday. We use all kinds of music forms in our services— rap, Southern Gospel, soft rock, hard rock, folk, Scripture songs—you name it. Our people here have a wide range of musical tastes, and we try hard to ac-commodate them all.

We have invested a lot of money in our music program. We have a state–of–the–art sound system, a 48–channel mixing board (with 48 wireless mikes), and a lighting system that matches anything you would find at a contemporary Christian artist concert. I can tell you this, if you have heard it on a contemporary Christian music radio station, we will probably be using it next Sunday!

We have a truly great worship band and lots of other talented people. Sure, we tend to cater to a younger crowd. Our median age around here is about 28 or 30. Older people don't tend to stay around very long for some reason. We do take some pride in that we don't have any hymnals. We believe the Lord wants us to use music that will speak to us where we are right now, not a bunch of songs that have ministered to our parents or grandparents.

The Only Our Brand of Worship is Right Church

I believe you have come to the right place if you want to learn what music and worship should be like in the church today. We believe we are following carefully the pattern of the early church. We believe in separating ourselves from anything that looks or sounds like the world. As the Apostle Paul wrote in 2 Corinthians 6:17 (KJV), "Come out from among them, and be ye separate, saith the Lord."

What kind of music do we use in our services? Well, I can tell you this, we don't use any of that contemporary junk some churches use. In fact, I know of only a few hymns we use that have been written since 1950. Our pastor has carefully examined every hymn in our church's hymnal and has concluded that only about 75 out of the 350 or so match up to the high theological and musical standards we hold here.

Sure, we have a choir and a solo or two in addition to congregational singing, but we believe the important thing in our services is the preaching. We view the music as a "warm–up" to what is really important in worship, the preaching of God's Word. Music helps to prepare people to receive what God will say to them through our pastor. We firmly believe that the world would be a much better place if all churches took our approach to worship.

The Only the Best is Good Enough for Us Church

Here at Only the Best Church, we believe that God is honored by musical proficiency. Not just anything is good enough for a God who is perfect! As Paul wrote in Philippians 1:10, "...approve the things that are excellent." Thus, in everything musical we do here, we are striving for excellence. In fact, I would go so far as to say that the better a performance is musically, the more spiritual it is, thus, the more it pleases God.

Our musical tastes here tend to be on the classical side. We have the largest pipe organ in town. In fact, our organist is chairperson of the organ department at a local music conservatory.

Our choir tries to live up to our church's name, Only the Best. People go through an extensive audition process just to become a member. We use a lot of anthems, choral responses, as well as four– and five–fold amens. Sure, it takes a lot of practice to be as good as we are, but is there anything too good for the Lord?

In fact, we are so committed to musical excellence, if we do not have people in our church who meet our high standards in a particular area, we have a budget large enough for us to pay for professionals to come in and enhance our choir and orchestra. We always have a lot of visitors, and we wouldn't want them to be disappointed with our music program.

The First Church of Blander is Better

You can probably tell by our name that we aren't the flashiest church around! No, we believe that we must take care not to worship in the flesh. That's why we never use anything but an organ and piano in our worship services. According to 1 Samuel 16:7, God is not looking at outward appearances.

We believe that God is pleased with consistency. That's why we jokingly say, "every service in exactly the same order—or your offering back." Why, we have people in our congregation who set their watches by when we sing the Doxology each week!

Our musical tastes are pretty middle-of-the-road, I would say. Nothing controversial here. We use the same hymnals we have had since the church was started 50 years ago. We work hard to not offend anyone. We sing only three verses of each hymn (first, second, and last), we have exactly four and a half minutes for the offertory, and we try our best to sing every hymn at about the same pace. We like to say that "if it hits the foot before it hits the heart, then it's probably too fast."

What Approach is Right?

So which of these approaches to music and worship is the best one? And, more importantly, which approach is biblical, if any? When it comes to what the Bible says about music and worship, each of these five churches is wrong—and right! You can probably discern the wrong things in these churches on your own, but there are at least three things that are right about how these five churches approached music and worship.

First, these churches are to be commended, at the very least, for having a strong emphasis on music and worship. Certainly each church took a different approach toward music and worship, but at least they understood music and worship should play an important part in the life of the local church. This textbook takes the position that music and worship are an absolutely vital part of the life of the local church. Regardless of the worship patterns you are currently using, the goal of this book is to encourage you to evaluate biblically what you believe about worship and to discover the wide range of worship activities that are, indeed, pleasing to God.

Second, each of the hypothetical ministers of music and worship had an understanding of their basic approach to music and worship. In other words, each had a philosophy of music and worship that somewhat guided their approach. You might disagree with some of their philosophies, but at least they were trying to answer the "why" questions. Why do we do worship this way? Why do we choose the particular songs we sing? Why do we structure our worship services the way we do? This textbook is not only interested in the *how* of music and worship, although we will deal with the how–to questions later in the book. I am also interested in challenging you to think about *why* your church worships like it does. And when you answer the "why" questions, you are dealing with your philosophy of music and worship.

Third, we can learn some things about music and worship from each of these churches. Each of them had their negative points, to be sure, but there were some positive ones, too! These hypothetical churches can teach us that it is futile to look for the "perfect" church after which we can model our music and worship. The perfect church does not exist. We can also seek to answer the question, "What can I learn, negatively and positively, from the worship practices of the churches I know about?" The study of the history of music and worship in the church is so important for this reason. By studying the strengths and weaknesses in worship practices for the past 2,000 years, we will be better equipped to structure a music and worship program that seeks to emphasize positive elements and eliminate negative ones.

In the following chapters we will examine how people worshiped in the Old and New Testaments, learn how people have applied music to worship in the 2,000 years since Pentecost, discover biblical principles of music and worship, and explore some very practical ways to apply them to the weekly life of your local church's worship program.

Jesus On Worship

We are not the only ones to face tough questions about approaches to worship. Jesus Himself faced it in His day. The background of John 4 is that Jesus and His disciples were traveling and had stopped for lunch at a well located outside the small town of Sychar. Jesus sent His disciples into town to buy some food, and while they were gone, He began speaking to a village woman who had come to the well for water. Jesus sought to capture her interest by speaking to her about "living water." Perhaps pointing to the well, Jesus said, "Everyone who drinks of this water shall thirst again; but whoever drinks of the water that I shall give him shall never thirst." Intrigued by Jesus' proclamation, the woman asked Him for the "living water" He was talking about. Jesus said, "Go, call your husband." "I have no husband," she said. Jesus agreed with her statement but then added that she actually had five husbands and noted the man she was currently living with was not her husband.

It was at this point, stung by Jesus' forthrightness, this woman sought to quickly change the subject. Seeking to divert Jesus' attention away from herself, she asked Him about the appropriate approach to worship. Expecting an argument, the woman was no doubt disarmed by Jesus' reply.

"Woman, believe Me, an hour is coming when neither in this mountain, nor in Jerusalem, shall you worship the Father...But an hour is coming, and now is, when the true worshipers shall worship the Father in spirit and truth; for such people the Father seeks to be His worshipers." Jesus in essence said to her, "Lady, neither the physical place of worship nor the form of worship is the main point. God is looking for people who will worship Him from their heart—in total honesty." Jesus emphasized the nature of worship is spiritual, not physical.

It is easy for any of us to get caught up in the forms of worship—how we sing and what we sing, the times and the places we do it, the variety of worship elements, and whose tastes and preferences we will honor. We can also find ourselves trapped in an unbending tradition or hopelessly confused by the raging winds of contemporary trends. But at the heart of worship is—the heart. Jesus reminded the Samaritan woman, and reminds us, worship is first and foremost a spiritual activity. While the forms, locations, and traditions of worship have their place, they are all fruitless without hearts that have been filled to overflowing with the living water that comes only from Jesus. To learn more about worship, one must start where Jesus did—the heart. When you turn your heart toward God with no hypocrisy or deceit, true worship will take place.

Worship in spirit and truth demands the full commitment of our total being. William Temple has eloquently written that "...to worship is to quicken the conscience by the holiness of God, to feed the mind with the truth of God, to purge the imagination by the beauty of God, to open the heart to the love of God, to devote the will to the purpose of God."

God desires for our worship of Him to focus solely on Him and not to be pulled away into arguments regarding the "best" style of worship.

A Picture of Worship in Spirit and Truth

I was raised in the home of a missionary. For the better part of my growing–up years, we lived in Alaska. Among their other ministries, my mother and father had the unique vision and desire to reach out to people with various types of disabilities. After several years, we had a good number of disabled people attending our church. If they could not get to church on their own, my father would pick them up in his aging station wagon.

The entire congregation was a picture of God's grace: an alcoholic turned deacon; a prostitute transformed into a Sunday School teacher; a blind man who taught an adult Sunday School class and played the piano for worship services; a young man, a former fugitive from the law, who helped to keep the church grounds; a young lady crippled from birth who greeted people at the door on Sunday mornings; a young man with Down's syndrome who helped take up the offering. All of these people were members of the kingdom of God and were serving God together to the best of their abilities. You can imagine the impact of such a congregation on a ten–year–old boy.

A tragic situation in this church, or so it seemed to me at the time, was a man and wife who had a daughter born with serious physical disabilities. She could not walk. She could not talk. Someone had to assist her in meeting all of her physical needs. She could not feed herself. She communicated by pointing to an alphabet printed on the slate she carried with her everywhere. She was home schooled because the school system had no provision for meeting the needs of someone in her condition. In spite of her limitations, my mother and dad shouldered the responsibility of transporting her to church every time the doors were open for services. Even then, she had to be strapped to her wheelchair so she would not fall over while in the car. Although her mom and dad bitterly blamed God for inflicting this plight on their family, this young girl was full of life and overflowed with joy. She had a genuine love for the Lord.

My father was a great one for having extended times of singing during the Sunday night services at our little church. My father entered the ministry during the 1940s when giant Youth for Christ rallies were held all over the country. He never lost the excitement of those rallies and their impact on his life. So, on almost every Sunday night our congregation resounded with an extended time of singing; usually simple choruses interchanged with spontaneous testimonies of praise.

On one such Sunday evening, I remember dad asking the congregation if anyone wanted to stand up and praise the Lord for His goodness. Suddenly, there was a rather significant stir from the middle of the congregation. I turned around to see this young girl slowly steering her wheelchair to the front of the church. About that time the converted alcoholic stepped over and helped her up to the area right in front of the pulpit. She motioned to my dad to come over to the wheelchair. By this time he was beginning to seriously question what was going on with his usually uneventful Sunday night service. The girl was undaunted. She spelled out on her alphabet slate her desire to sing a solo. My father looked dumbfounded. How could this girl, except for a few groans and guttural sounds, expect to make any kind of music with her lips to the Lord? My dad asked her what she wanted to sing. She pointed to the hymn "Amazing Grace" in her open hymnal. My father turned to the blind pianist and said, "Jimmy, can you play 'Amazing Grace'? We have someone special to sing for us tonight." Jimmy played a brief introduction and she began to make groans and moanings in time with the music. I was not able to clearly understand a word she sang. But somehow the musicianship and articulation of words did not matter. All of us understood intuitively what she was doing and more importantly—why she was doing it. There was no doubt. We all knew she was singing from her heart to the living God. There was not a dry eye in the audience. Even the children were captured and stilled by the moment. And, I am certain God was honored to be praised. That young girl, I believe, was worshiping God in spirit and in truth.

God does not want us to focus on fancy music programs. He wants us to focus on Him! He does not desire for us to aim for a perfect performance alone. He desires us to aim for a perfect heart before Him. He does not want us to set our hearts on well–organized music programs, new hymnals, state–of–the–art sound systems, expensive instruments, or magnificent choirs and practice rooms. He wants us to set our hearts on Him. He does not demand for us to sing only when we can do so with wonderful sound tracks or huge, live orchestras. He does demand from us songs of praise, sung from a heart of love, adoration, and thankfulness. He is looking for musicians who will walk with Him, fellowship with Him, and work unselfishly for Him.

To Sum It Up

There are as many worship styles as there are churches. There is no one pattern of worship that is right for every church. Rather, we can learn, both from church history and our own experiences, positive and negative points about many styles of worship. Jesus taught that worship begins in the heart of the worshiper, not in the place or form of worship.

For Further Discussion

1. What are the strengths and weaknesses of each of the five hypothetical churches?
2. What does it mean to worship "in truth"?
3. Share with the class your own most memorable time of worship.

For Application

1. What is your church's worship style? Which of the five hypothetical churches is most like your church and why?
2. Evaluate the music and worship approach at your church. What are its strengths? What are its weaknesses?
3. What are some specific ways your church could encourage worship from the heart?

Worship and the
Great Commission

2

*If Socrates would enter the room we should rise and do him
honor. But if Jesus Christ came into the room we should fall down
on our knees and worship Him.* —Napoleon Bonaparte

Imagine that your very best friend is the King of the Universe.
For the past three years you have walked with Him every day. Each
new day is the unfolding of another adventure—sitting at His feet
captivated by His every word, watching Him reach down to lift children on His lap, marveling as He performs miracles, believing Him
when He says, "I am the way, and the truth, and the life" (John
14:6). Since you met Jesus, your life has completely changed.

Imagine eating meals with Jesus, sharing accommodations with
Him, watching Him disrupt the trade of the moneychangers in the
temple, rebuke the religious leaders, weep over Jerusalem, and proph-
esy His own impending death. Imagine that you were with Him in
the upper room, sharing the Passover with Him, having your feet
washed by Him, singing with Him, listening carefully to His words,
and walking with Him to the Garden of Gethsemane. You have come
to love and reverence Jesus more with each passing day. You cannot
imagine life without Him.

Then, it happens. Within the space of 12 hours, your world is
violently rearranged. You find yourself running in fear for your life,
Jesus is arrested, put on trial, and crucified. You learn from John
that Jesus is dead—and it seems that all of your hopes and dreams
have died with Him.

But something marvelous, amazing, radical, and history–trans-
forming takes place three days later. At first, it was Mary and a handful of other woman who were told by an angel at Jesus' tomb "He is
not here, for He has risen, just as He said . . . go quickly and tell His
disciples . . ." (Matt. 28:6, 7). Their words seemed too wonderful to
be true. Everyone knew that Jesus was dead! But it was not long
until it happened! While you and the disciples were in a room be-

hind locked doors, the resurrected Jesus appeared. Your reaction? Matthew recalled "they came up and took hold of His feet and worshiped Him" (Matt. 28:9). Worship!

The 28th chapter of Matthew is immediately recognized by Christians as containing the last words of Jesus before His ascension—widely known as the *Great Commission*. What many believers overlook is that before the disciples heard Jesus' words regarding the power, proclamation, and promise of the Church's mission, the disciples were involved with worship!

> But the eleven disciples proceeded to Galilee, to the mountain which Jesus had designated. And when they saw Him, they worshiped Him; but some were doubtful. And Jesus came up and spoke to them, saying, "All authority has been given to Me in heaven and on earth. Go therefore and make disciples of all the nations, baptizing them in the name of the Father and the Son and the Holy Spirit, teaching them to observe all that I commanded you; and, lo, I am with you always, even to the end of the age." (Matt. 28:16–20)

It must have been one of those incredibly busy days when Jesus told His disciples to meet Him in Galilee. One of those gut–wrenching kind of days when the pressure seems overwhelming—all you want to do is to go home and hide. No doubt the disciples were exhausted. Jesus had been with them for forty days since His resurrection. The time had been crammed with important teaching about the kingdom of God and the role each of them was to play in it (Acts 1:3). The disciples were probably not excited about climbing up some mountain top. But in spite of their weariness of mind and body, Jesus placed His disciples in an environment where they had to focus on two things: worshiping Him and listening to His words.

Jesus knew the time had come to leave His disciples. He also knew His departure would be traumatic and unsettling for them. And yet, Jesus wanted to leave them with final instructions which would guide and direct their energies in the coming years. Jesus decided to leave His disciples with a "mission statement" not only for them, but for the entire Church. However, the disciples were not ready to receive this mission statement until they had first opened their hearts to God in worship. So it is with Christians today. For us to clearly hear and respond to Christ's commands regarding our ministry responsibilities for world evangelization and edification, we must first come to Him in worship.

What is Worship?

But, what does it mean to worship? For many people, worship is something that is done on Sunday mornings in a church building. To them, it may involve many elements: music, liturgy, prayers, offerings, choirs, solos, instrumental music, Scripture reading, and preaching. Certainly all of these items can be part of worshiping God. But in its simplest form, worship is individually telling God you love Him. It is the act of loving God. It is intense devotion and admiration of God. It is communicating with the living God. Worship is what nurtures our relationship with God. Worship is rejoicing in the fact that God is your Friend, Redeemer, Comforter, Companion, Sovereign, Provider, Healer, Giver of Life, and Peace.

The word *worship* comes from the Anglo–Saxon *weorthscipe* which meant to "ascribe worth, to pay homage, to reverence or venerate." The word was modified to *worthship* and then to what we use today, *worship*. What a person values (or places a high worth upon) is what will be worshiped.

Praise, an integral part of worship, is the act of bragging on God. The word "praise" itself means to express approval or admiration. Praise involves setting a price, a value of worth and extreme approval. It is telling God He is your God and He alone deserves honor, glory, majesty, and power. When we praise God, we are giving Him our commendation, approval, admiration, glorification, and applause. We are telling God He is great and wonderful. Praise is acknowledging to God, and the world around you, that He is Creator, All–Powerful, Sustainer, Eternal, Holy, and Righteous.

Why Worship?

Why worship? If all the angels in heaven are constantly surrounding God with songs of worship, then why does He need His children on earth to worship Him as well? There are at least four reasons why we should worship God.

First, we have been commanded to worship God. The first of the Ten Commandments states it in the negative: "I *am* the LORD your God, who brought you out of the land of Egypt, out of the house of slavery. You shall have no other gods before Me" (Exod. 20:2, 3) or as it is restated in Exodus 34:14, "for you shall not worship any other god, for the Lord, whose name *is* Jealous, *is* a jealous God."

Second, worship is necessary because it takes the focus off ourselves and directs it to God, acknowledging that He is the Sovereign Lord of the universe and our lives. Jesus wanted the disciples to center their attention on Him and upon what He was about to say.

Third, worship prepares us to receive God's Word. People who practice a life of worship are people who are also listening carefully to God. When they hear God's Word, they will obey it.

Fourth, the practice of worship provides us the opportunity to look at all of life through the lenses of worship. In other words, as we focus on God (taking the focus off of ourselves and our circumstances) and focus on His Word, we will begin to see the rest of life as God sees it—as it really is. The more we worship God, the more clearly we are able to view our lives from His perspective.

Jesus knew that after His departure the disciples would face many and varied difficulties and obstacles as they sought to carry out His commands. He also knew that through the practice of worship, the disciples would be able to face hardship, difficulty, persecution, and even death victoriously, because their primary focus would be on God and their relationship with Him.

Where Do We Worship?

A place for worship is both unimportant and important. It is unimportant in that Jesus taught it could be done anywhere and anytime (John 4:21–24). However, the location of worship is important in the sense that using a place away from the normal frenzied activities of the average person's life can be very helpful in experiencing true worship. Note these two facts from Matthew 28—the disciples went away and they went away to an appointed place.

During Jesus' earthly ministry, people were always clamoring for His attention. To counter this, at least nine times the Gospels record Jesus going away (or at least trying to), arising early before dawn to pray, or spending time alone "in the wilderness." Part of preparing for worship is shutting out the rest of life and focusing attention on meeting with God. Satan has many cunning ways of distracting God's children so they just do not make the time to be with their heavenly Father. Without taking the step of "going away" to a place designated for worship, we may find worship to be difficult, if not impossible. Jesus knew the disciples needed to shut out the rest of the world in order to carefully focus their hearts, minds and souls, first—on Jesus' person and second—on Jesus' words.

For us today, the first step toward worship is to find (or make) a place that is accessible, quiet, away from the press of the daily grind— a place where we can focus our entire attention upon God, who He is, and what He means to us. Thus, worship must become a personal priority. Worship happened for the disciples as they "went away." The word for "went away" *(poreuomai)* means to follow someone. The disciples were following Jesus to Galilee and, by the act of following, they were making worship a priority. For worship to be a priority in your life, you must be committed to following Jesus, even when He seems to be leading you off of the beaten path.

The disciples not only "went away" following Jesus, they were following Jesus to a particular place. We know from Jesus' frequent use of the Garden of Gethsemane there were places which were special to Jesus. It is clear that Jesus choose ("designated") this meeting place. It is not enough simply to get away from the noise and clamor of daily life—we must find a place and time to meet with God. This principle is true for private and public worship.

When Do We Worship?

Matthew writes, "when they saw Him, they worshiped Him." Worship takes place as the believer looks to Jesus and sees Him for who He really is—King of Kings and Lord of Lords. The disciples saw Jesus—they saw Him as their risen Lord, their Messiah, their Living Sacrifice, their Advocate with the Father. Christ did not speak to the disciples until they first saw Him and then worshiped Him.

But the word "saw" here means more than just seeing with one's physical eyes. It means "to know" as well. Before the disciples worshiped Jesus, they had to know Him—to understand exactly who He was. Isaiah was moved to repentance when He "saw" the Lord high and lifted up (Isa. 6:1). In Luke 24, the two men walking on the road to Emmaus met Jesus and at the end of their journey "their eyes were opened and they recognized Him" (Luke 24:31). John records that Peter "saw and believed" (John 20:8). The women who went to the tomb early Sunday morning, to find it empty, hurried away to tell the disciples what they had seen. On the way, they were met by Jesus. Their immediate response? They "took hold of His feet and worshiped Him" (Matt. 28:9). Seeing Jesus and, in that seeing, recognizing who He is, always leads to worship!

We will not be able to see Jesus with our physical eyes until we see Him in heaven, but when our spiritual eyes are opened by the miracle of new birth and we see Jesus through the eyes of faith, we hear from God. When we see Jesus as our Savior, Redeemer, Risen Lord, and Coming King, and we are moved to worship Him—then He will speak to us. The biblical principle, in both testaments, is that those who see God for who He is will respond to Him in worship.

Doubters and Worship

In the midst of the disciples worshiping Jesus on a mountaintop in Galilee, Matthew tells us that "some were doubtful." It may be hard to imagine being in the presence of the resurrected Son of

God and having doubts, but that is exactly what happened. Some might have doubted what they were seeing was real—perhaps it was only a dream. Maybe some thought that it was not really Jesus, but an imposter. Thus, it should not surprise us when we find ourselves in public worship and it seems that everyone is not on the same wave length. If "doubt" could take place among the disciples in the very presence of Jesus, it can certainly happen with us today. But while Matthew tells us that doubt was present that day, Jesus did not rebuke those who were doubting. He did not ask the doubters to go home. Instead, Jesus shared with them, doubter and non–doubter alike, the Word of God—His Word—the *Great Commission*.

Worship and the Word

It was after the disciples worshiped that Jesus spoke to them. We will never experience the wonder of Jesus speaking to us until we open the pathway of communication through worship. Jesus spoke in spite of the doubters. He will do so today. If we focus on worshiping Christ, loving Him with all of our hearts, living in submission to Him in motive and deed, He will speak to us. The primary way God speaks to us today is through the reading, teaching, and preaching of the Word of God. But God may also speak to us through music, through other believers, or through the "small still voice" of our circumstances. Regardless of the method, God will speak to us when we worship Him.

Immediately after the disciples worshiped, Jesus reminded them of the authority given Him by the Father. Jesus then challenged them to make disciples of all nations. They were to reproduce themselves by going, baptizing, and teaching them to observe (not just to know) all things He had commanded the disciples. And then Jesus gave them words to give them hope in the dark times, "I am with you always, *even* to the end of the age." The worship of the disciples led them to receive the word of the Master—words of empowerment (v. 18), challenge (v. 19, 20a), and encouragement (v. 20b). But the worship of the disciples did not stop at a mountain in Galilee. The books of Acts through Revelation record that the disciples continued to worship and faithfully carried out the *Great Commission* Christ had given them. So it will be with us. Those who truly worship God will faithfully carry out His commands.

Personal Worship

The great news is this—you do not have to just imagine your very best friend is the King of Universe! If you are a believer in Jesus Christ, you already have a personal relationship with Him. If you are not a believer—you can become one! The key to unlocking that relationship is the key of worship. Like the disciples in Matthew 28, you must get away. Second, you should establish an appointed place where you will meet with God on a daily basis. Third, you must acknowledge that Jesus is the resurrected Son of God. Jesus must become the focus of your life and your worship. Fourth, as you worship and God speaks to you through His Word, your response must involve obedience to His commands. Fifth, as you walk in worship and obedience, you will be filled with the assurance of His presence in every aspect of your life.

Marty Funderburk has expressed well the joys of a lifelong relationship with Jesus which is cultivated through worship in the song, *When We Praise*:

There is hope,
there is peace,
there's a place of release,
when we praise, when we praise the Father.
Deliverance from sin,
a cleansing within,
when we praise, praise the name of Jesus.
A fresh anointing and a heart renewed by faith,
there is healing for the hurting when we praise.

When we praise
we open wide the windows of heaven;
when we praise,
His grace is outpoured;
when we raise our hearts together in cries of worship,
miracles can happen, when we praise the Lord.

There is passion restored for loving the Lord when we praise.
When we praise the Father,
the nations will see and many will believe.
When we praise, praise the name of Jesus,
when we exalt Him to His high and rightful place.
He is honored,
He is worshiped when we praise.

Until eternity,
my one desire will be,
may the rest of my life be a sweet sacrifice
of praise to my Lord Jesus Christ.

To Sum It Up

The focus of this book is on the role of music and worship in the local church. The starting point of corporate worship begins with each individual's commitment to Jesus as Lord and Savior and a desire to be involved regularly in personal worship. Involvement in personal worship will then lead to meaningful times of corporate worship.

For Further Discussion

1. What are some other reasons to worship God, in addition to the four reasons given in the text?
2. What are some obstacles to worship that people face today?
3. What are other biblical examples of worship not mentioned in this chapter?
4. What are some reasons church attenders might "doubt" today?
5. What additional results of worship will be observed in the life of the individual believer and the life of the local church?

For Application

1. What would you do differently in your private worship times if Jesus met with you as He did with His disciples?
2. What would be different about corporate worship at your church if next Sunday Jesus was going to preach the sermon?
3. Use your church's hymnal to locate songs which mention worship in some way. What is being taught in these songs about worship?
4. What are the strong points and weak points of your personal devotional time? What have you learned from this chapter which can help you improve the weak points?
5. What are some principles of worship from this chapter which can be applied to family worship?

An Old Testament Recipe for Music & Worship

3

*Worship is the act of rising to a personal, experimental conscious-
ness of the real presence of God which floods the soul with joy and
bathes the whole inward spirit with refreshing streams of life.*
—Rufus Matthew Jones

It was an early Sunday morning in June. My family of four piled
into our car to attend our first of two worship services. Although the
sun was bright, the air was cool. I had forgotten what summer mornings could be like in Canada. I had just completed a week of directing the music for a church conference in New Brunswick. At the
conference I had been asked by one of the local pastors to speak in
the Sunday morning services of his two, small churches, where he
served on a part–time basis. As we drove to the first congregation, I
was mentally reviewing my message and my wife was humming
through the music we had selected to sing during the service.

We arrived fifteen minutes before the service was to begin and
noted there were only a few cars in the parking lot. I met the pastor
on the front steps to greet people as they arrived, while my wife went
in to check on the piano.

In a few minutes, I entered the building with the pastor and
walked to the front. Including my family and the pastor, there were
only 17 in attendance. In the background, an elderly lady was playing *Love Lifted Me* on what seemed to be the most out–of–tune piano in North America.

There we stood: my family of four dressed in our Sunday best,
the elderly husband of the pianist, a young man trying to hold three
children on his lap, a couple near retirement age, a younger couple
with two children, and the pastor. I was not impressed. We began
singing *Love Lifted Me*. My heart sank. Not only was the piano out of
tune, the congregation was too! How could I worship when the music
was this bad? How could my wife and I sing after this? How could I
preach after this? How could the Lord meet with a congregation

21

who seemed to be satisfied with mediocrity in what I considered to be one of the most important elements of worship—the music?

But as I was sorting through my negative feelings, something remarkable began to take place. At the beginning of the second verse, I saw the husband of the pianist begin to weep quietly. Then, I saw the young man with the three kids reach into his pocket for his handkerchief. Apparently, he too was having an emotional experience of some kind. I looked across the aisle to see the pastor, so overcome with emotion that he stopped singing.

This kind of response continued during the second hymn. It seemed somehow the music that sounded so bad to me was actually improving. What was going on here? When the hymn was over, the pastor asked the congregation, "Does anybody here have a witness?"

The first to speak was the young man with the three small children. He said he wanted to publicly praise God for being so good to him. He told of getting up early, dressing his children, and arriving at the small church building without any assistance from his wife. She was not a believer and did not want any part of this "religion stuff." He praised the Lord for saving him out of a life of drug and alcohol abuse.

After the young father finished, the husband of the pianist stood and praised the Lord for changing his life more than 50 years earlier, telling of his desire to know the fullness of God. Then the pianist stood and thanked God for the opportunity to play the piano. She shared her desire for God use her limited abilities for His glory. The pastor asked the congregation to bow their heads and pray silently as he called out the various names of God. Then, one by one, he brought requests of the congregants before the Lord. As I listened, I found myself forgetting about the size of the congregation or the quality of their music—I was thinking about God! These people were worshiping God and I found myself worshiping, too!

Ingredient One—Sing to the Lord

As I have reflected on this experience, I believe the congregation was simply practicing the recipe for worship given to us centuries ago in Psalm 96:

Sing to the Lord a new song;
Sing to the Lord, all the earth. (Ps. 96:1)

This recipe contains five major ingredients which, when combined, will produce a God–honoring worship experience. The first ingredient is that we are to sing to the Lord. But why does God command us to sing? Why are we told to sing to the Lord and not to other people? What is the new song we are supposed to be singing?

Why singing?

One of God's greatest gifts to humanity is the gift of song. In its purest sense, singing is communication. God has given us this gift to use not just to communicate with other people but primarily to communicate with Him. One of God's motivations for creating us was so we could have fellowship with Him. Singing is one of the ways human beings can express their emotions to God and enter into fellowship with Him.

Why sing to the Lord?

Singing to God prohibits us from making worship a spectator event. It might be possible for someone visiting a worship service on any particular Sunday to think the choir and soloists are singing to the congregation. Thus, the congregation becomes merely an audience. But the biblical picture is to realize God is the audience. All the music, whether congregational, choral, or featured groups, should be directed Godward.

Singing is one of the creative gifts God has given every man, woman, and child. That does not mean God has given each person equal musical ability. But God has given all persons the capability of lifting their voices in praise to Him—regardless of the "quality" of the presentation. This does not mean that we should not care about the quality of our music or that God is satisfied with second–best efforts or worse. It simply means God is primarily listening to the song of the heart, not the song of the voice.

Why sing a new song?

The psalmist did not say to sing a good song or an artistically well–crafted song. Psalm 96 did not say to sing a song that meets the expectations of others, nor to sing a song with a great melody. We are simply told to sing to the Lord a new song! God does not want worn–out phrases which have lost their meaning. He desires us to have a fresh expression of our experience with Him. God does not want our leftovers. He wants our best, most creative moments and purest motives. He does not want our insincere, hurried gestures of love. He desires each individual to focus attention solely upon Him.

Who is to sing?

Everyone and everything is to praise the Creator! All the earth! The psalmist mentions the heavens, the earth, the sea, the field, and "all the trees of the forest" as praising God by their very existence. We, as being created in God's image, have the joy of choosing to praise God. God does not place any qualifiers on who is to sing to

Him. It is not just those who are talented, trained, or accomplished musicians. Everyone is to sing. God is looking for people who will respond to Him by singing a "new song"—a new song of praise for who He is and what He has done. Worship is not an option—it is a commandment.

Ingredient Two—Proclaim His Wonders

Tell of His glory among the nations,
His wonderful deeds among all the peoples.
For great is the Lord, and greatly to be praised;
He is to be feared above all gods.
For all the gods of the peoples are idols,
But the Lord made the heavens.
Splendor and majesty are before Him,
Strength and beauty are in His sanctuary. (Ps. 96:3–6)

The second ingredient in worship is to share the wonders of God with those around us—to praise Him. This is the act of praising God to the unbeliever and believer alike. We are commanded to declare the "glory of the Lord" to the "nations" and His "wonderful deeds" to "all the peoples." Too often Christians are busy telling about the wonderful things they have done for God instead of what God has done for them. Although some may find it difficult to tell other people about the wonders of God, it is a clear commandment to those who would worship Him.

There are many ways to praise the Lord during a worship service. We can praise the Lord through a word of testimony, a song of praise, a report from a mission field, or through the use of instrumental music. Music, without words, can express feelings of praise which cannot be fully expressed with words.

We are to communicate our testimonies of what God has done in our lives to two groups: "the nations" and "all the peoples." "The nations," also translated "the heathen," refers to those who do not know the Lord. We are to "proclaim good tidings of His salvation from day to day." The true proclamation of what God has done in our lives and the lives of others can be used by God to draw those who are not part of His family to Himself. "The peoples" refers to the people of God. Sharing publicly what God has done in our lives is not just evangelistic but also edifying. As we hear what God is doing in the lives of our brothers and sisters, we in turn are challenged to examine how He is working in our own lives and moved to praise Him ourselves.

One of the best examples telling God's wonderful deeds among His children is found in Psalm 136. The psalmist gives a step–by–

step historical recounting of all the ways God intervened on behalf of the children of Israel. The psalmist reminded the people of how good God had been to them through His mighty miracles. The psalmist started at creation, then detailed God's deliverance of the children of Israel from Egypt and their victories in the land of promise. As a clear testimony to God's role in each event, the psalmist concludes each statement of victory with "For His lovingkindness is everlasting."

When we give God credit for all He has done, before the unbeliever and believer, we take attention away from ourselves and focus it on the very one responsible for "every good thing . . . and every perfect gift" (James 1:17). When we see God as the giver of all good things, we are drawn closer to God and people. We are encouraged and uplifted as we are reminded of how God prepares, plans, and provides for His own.

Ingredient Three—Give to the Lord

Ascribe to the Lord, O families of the peoples, Ascribe to the Lord glory and strength. Ascribe to the Lord the glory of His name; Bring an offering, and come into His courts. (Ps. 96:7, 8)

The third ingredient in worship involves the giving to the Lord of strength, honor, glory and an offering. Giving and worship are inseparable. When we give to God out of the right motivation, we are worshiping. When we truly worship God, we will be motivated to give. Jack R. Taylor says in his book, *The Hallelujah Factor*, "It (giving) is elicited by praise and elicits further praise. There may be giving without praise, but there cannot be praise without giving. True praise is always accompanied by giving."

What is giving?

Giving is providing tangible evidence of our love and appreciation to God as Sovereign, Redeemer, Comforter, and Provider. We show this appreciation anytime we give of our money, our labors, and our talents. God does not need our money—He already owns the universe. God does not need our energy or tireless labors. He holds more energy in the smallest atom than we could generate in a lifetime of service. God does not need our talents. Not only does God enjoy the talents of millions of angels to praise Him but He can empower even the rocks to praise Him if He so chooses (Luke 19:40). God has asked us to give to Him not because of what He needs but because of what it demands from us. To give in a spirit of worship demands we acknowledge that all we have belongs to God. We have a responsibility to share with Him part of what He has given to us.

How are we to give?

A familiar passage in Romans 12:1 gives insight into our need to give to the Lord as part of our worship. Paul wrote, "I urge you therefore, brethren, by the mercies of God, to present your bodies a living and holy sacrifice, acceptable to God, which is your spiritual service of worship." Even in the Old Testament, God desired more than offerings of lambs and cattle. Here in the New Testament it is clear—the sacrifice God desires most of all is everything we have. He wants us!

Here are some principles which should guide our giving in worship. First, God owns everything. Thus, everything we have, even things we may think we have earned, belong to Him. As believers, we are merely stewards of what He has given us (1 Cor. 4:2).

Second, we are to give to the *Lord*. Our focus in giving should not be our church, a denomination, a pet project, or to make ourselves look good in the sight of others. We are giving to the Lord.

Third, we are to give out of the proper motivation. God is more concerned about why we give than what we give (see Mark 12:41–44; 1 Cor. 13; and 2 Cor. 9:7).

Fourth, God wants us to give ourselves totally to Him, not just our money or our time. Worship demands a total commitment on the part of the worshiper. God desires those who will say to Him as Isaac Watts expressed in his classic hymn, *When I Survey the Wondrous Cross*:

Were the whole realm of nature mine,
That were a present far too small;
Love so amazing, so divine,
Demands my soul, my life, my all.

Ingredient Four—Holiness Before the Lord

Worship the Lord in holy attire;
Tremble before Him, all the earth. (Ps. 96:9)

The fourth ingredient in worship is that the worshiper must come before the Lord "in holy attire" or as the King James translates it, "in the beauty of holiness." There are two aspects of how we are to come before the Lord. First, the only way anyone can come into God's presence in "holy attire" is to come through the blood of Jesus. The writer of Hebrews describes this wonderful truth in 10:19–22. When we place our trust in Jesus and are born into the kingdom of God, we are accepted as holy in God's sight—just as holy as Jesus!

Second, "holy attire" also refers to a consciousness of our own sinfulness and the need to regularly confess our sins to God. When we trust Christ for salvation, we are assured a place in heaven. Jesus died for the sins of the world (1 John 2:2)—past, present, and future—and when we trust him, all sins are covered, past, present, and future. But unconfessed sin can hinder our communication with God and the ability to freely worship Him. Thus, we should do a spiritual inventory every time we enter into the presence of God, privately or publicly, and confess our sins (1 John 1:9).

My wife is a nurse. She is constantly reminding me an open sore or wound is contaminated by the outside environment and must be sterilized before healing will begin to take place. This principle is of critical importance when a patient undergoes surgery. For any surgery to be successful, there must be an unpolluted environment in the operating room. Any germ or virus, all of which are microscopic, can mean disaster for the patient. So it is with the person who is entering the presence of a holy God. Any unconfessed sin, no matter how small, can keep us from experiencing the fellowship of His presence. But as we trust Christ for spiritual cleansing, God allows us into His presence because our sin and guilt are covered by the blood of Jesus. Through Christ we are fitted with the "holy attire" God requires.

Ingredient Five—Proclaim the Word of the Lord

Say among the nations, "The Lord reigns;
Indeed, the world is firmly established, it will not be moved;
He will judge the peoples with equity."
Let the heavens be glad, and let the earth rejoice;
Let the sea roar, and all it contains;
Let the field exult, and all that is in it.
Then all the trees of the forest will sing for joy
Before the Lord, for He is coming;
For He is coming to judge the earth.
He will judge the world in righteousness,
And the peoples in His faithfulness. (Ps. 96:10–13)

The fifth ingredient in the recipe for worship is to proclaim the Word of the Lord. True worship always results in the sharing of God's message with "the nations." True worship does not begin and end in the confines of a church sanctuary. Worship must begin in the heart of the individual believer and will continue as the Word of God is shared with the world.

The message we are to share is multi–dimensional. First, we are to share truth about the person of God. God is the sovereign Lord who created the universe and is now ruling over it. Nothing can happen without His direction or permission.

Second, we are to proclaim truth about the coming judgment of God. This is a clear foreshadowing of the second coming of Christ. Jesus will bodily return to planet Earth. And when He does, God will judge each individual, and His judgment will be fair and just (v. 10, 13). Our message must be one of warning ("prepare to meet thy God") and one of hope ("if any man be in Christ he is a new creation").

Third, we are to proclaim the truth that all creation was brought into existence to praise God and bring glory to Him. Every planet, every star, every galaxy, and every individual human being was brought into existence for the primary purpose of worshiping God!

To Sum It Up

I will never forget that small congregation in New Brunswick. That day, God used His people to turn my mind away from what I could find wrong with the service to focus on worship—where it should have been all along.

That group of believers taught me God wants us to sing every song to Him as one which is brand new. I learned God is not necessarily glorified by the size of a crowd but He is always glorified when one believer publicly praises the Lord for who He is and what He has done. A piano player taught me the joy of giving to the Lord—unselfishly, reverently, obediently. A humble pastor taught me the importance of simple, straightforward intercession for the needs of people. As the Word was proclaimed, they responded joyfully and left that tiny auditorium to live for God another week. And as my family and I got in the car to leave, I realized they had taught me what it meant to really worship God.

For Further Discussion

1. What are some situations in which you have found it difficult to worship God? How can those situations be turned into times of worship?
2. What are the hymns you find yourself thinking of during times of stress? Times of joy? Why do those particular hymns come to your mind?
3. List some ways Christians can express worship through giving.

For Application

1. Write down on a sheet of paper the items for which you are thankful. Using those items, write out your praise to God in complete sentences. Sing those sentences back to God using a familiar melody or one you make up. You have just written a "new song" to the Lord!
2. Structure an order of service using the pattern of Psalm 96.
3. Write a brief account of a worship experience that taught you some valuable lessons about worship.

Survey of Music & Worship: Old Testament Foundations

4

Worship is a way of living, a way of seeing the world in the light of God. To worship is to rise to a higher level of existence, to see the world from the point of view of God. —Abraham J. Herschel

God's people have always been lovers of song. Throughout the pages of the Old Testament, God's people have expressed their joy, gratitude, praise, adoration, sorrow, sadness, determination, and dedication through music. According to Strong's Concordance, music (also musick in the KJV) or singing is mentioned over 60 times (KJV). The word *sing* is used over 120 times. The words *singer* and *singers* are recorded over 40 times. *Musical* or *musician* are recorded over 50 times. The morning stars sang together in Job 38 and the first record of the Hebrew people joining together in songs of praise is found in Exodus 15:1.

The Beginning of Music

Music is first described in sacred history in Genesis 4:20, 21. This passage introduces two brothers, Jabal and Jubal. Jabal is described as a cattle breeder while Jubal is called "The father of all who play the lyre and pipe." His occupation as a maker of music is defined as a trade along side that of his brother, the cattleman. No mention is made as to whether Jubal's early musical practices were sacred or secular.

In the Old Testament, music was used to accompany work, worship, merrymaking, war, and more. Exodus 15:1, 2 describes the first recorded instance of singing praise to the Lord. Moses praised God in song in Deuteronomy 32:3. Joshua and Gideon used trumpets at the time of battle and the choir preceded the army of God when Jehoshaphat went into battle (2 Chron. 20:21, 22).

Occasions when music was used in the Old Testament include a family party for Jacob in Genesis 31, a celebration at the crossing of the Red Sea in Exodus 15, the welcome of Jephthah in Judges 11:34, and the triumph of David in 1 Samuel 18:6. In 2 Samuel 22, songs of praise to the name of Jehovah are sung among the nations. First Chronicles 16:8–10 is a song of thanksgiving written by Asaph and delivered by King David. Job 36 refers to man praising the work of God in song. Isaiah used song to encourage the worship of Jehovah (Isa. 42) and Jonah sang songs of thanksgiving at his deliverance from the belly of the great fish (Jonah 2:9).

Music was used to inspire prophets, enthrone kings, celebrate the harvest, exorcise evil spirits, and celebrate weddings. It was used for dirges and lamentation, magic and incantations, feasting and occupation. But the most significant use of music in the Old Testament was in praising Jehovah God.

The Psalms

God provided a hymnal of *praises* for His people that today we call the Psalms. From the time of David on, the Psalms were used as an integral part of Hebrew worship. In the truest sense, the Psalms are a poetic dialogue between God and man which was set to music. This book gave the Hebrew worshiper opportunity to praise God through music. It was used to provide offerings of songs to accompany the other offerings of sacrifices. Psalms, performed by the temple musicians, were sung when the temple of Solomon was built, and clearly represented the entire span of man's relationship with God.

The Book of Psalms is divided into five sections also referred to as "books": Book I—Psalms 1–41; Book II—Psalms 42–72; Book III—Psalms 73–89; Book IV—Psalms 90–106; and Book V—Psalms 107–150. The five divisions were written to correspond with the first five books of the Old Testament written by Moses, also called the Pentateuch. Included in the collection are: Psalms of Praise, Psalms of History, Psalms of Penitence, Psalms of Imprecation (cursing of enemies), and Messianic Psalms (prophetic regarding the coming of Christ as Messiah). It should be noted that the Psalms include more than 175 references of praise for God's greatness, justice, wonders, compassion, mercy, grace, righteousness, and protection which are to be sung in worship to God. The instruction in Psalm 7:17 is to sing praise to the name of the Lord. Psalms 9, 13, 16, 18, 40, and 59 are songs of praise and thanksgiving to God for His goodness, sovereign care, salvation, strength, and protection. Instructions to make music skillfully on a variety of instruments are given in Psalm 33.

Hebrew Music Prior to King David

Music in Hebrew worship was inseparable from everyday life. Music making was specifically connected to the mighty acts of God.

Music in the tabernacle was not as well defined as it would be subsequently in the temple. Because of the nomadic life generally associated with early Hebrew culture, worship music prior to King David's reign was probably unstructured and little more than the ringing of cymbals, blowing of trumpets, and spontaneous noise–making. Even so, musical presentations took the form of vocal solos, small ensembles, congregational singing, choir, instrumental offerings, and dance accompanied by voice or instrument. Much music making was by non–professional women, choral musicians, and dancers. The song of Moses (Exod. 15) celebrating victory over Egypt was followed by Miriam playing the tambourine while leading women singers and dancers. Women sang to King David in 1 Samuel 18 and in Judges 11 Jephthah's daughter sang, danced, and played instruments upon the return of her father from battle.

Music and Worship for the Temple

King David is credited with structuring music for temple worship. In fact, more than 10 percent of the people serving in temple ministries were musicians. David appointed 4,000 members of the 38,000 member tribe of Levi to serve as professional ministers of music and singers. Their responsibilities included playing "with instruments of music, harps, lyres, and loud-sounding cymbals, to raise sounds of joy" (1 Chron. 15:16). Music leaders were selected (divided into 24 orders of 12) for the purpose of assisting in teaching and training temple musicians.

Patterns for Music Leadership

King David placed Chenaniah as leader of song (1 Chron. 15:22). Chenaniah in turn appointed three men and their sons to take charge of all the responsibilities pertaining to worship music. Heman, Asaph, and Jeduthun were appointed as leaders to teach and train musicians to serve as singers, percussionists, and players of wind instruments (1 Chron. 25:1–7).

Heman and his sons were responsible for leading singers and instrumentalists (1 Chron. 15:19). Jeduthun and his sons were responsible for those playing with cymbals and percussion instruments (2 Chron. 5:12). Asaph and his sons were directly responsible for teaching and training musicians.

Asaph and his sons stand as a testimony of talented musicians. He wrote 12 of the 150 Psalms, led in the organization of a music school for the purpose of instructing others, and served as director of music on the day King Solomon dedicated the temple and "the glory of the Lord filled the house" (2 Chron. 7:1). Asaph was both musician and theologian. He wrote about the lostness of humankind (Ps. 74:20), the cure for trouble (Ps. 77:2–20), the struggle between prosperity and envy (Ps. 73), and the wealth appropriated for the child of God (Ps. 50:10). It was Psalm 82:6, written by Asaph, that Jesus quoted when defending His own deity to doubting religious leaders (John 10:34). Asaph's sons followed in their father's footsteps. They rose out of the 70–year Babylonian tyranny and sang their way from Babylon to Jerusalem. The sons of Asaph led the music at the foundation dedication for the second temple (Ezra 2:1, 36–38, 40, 41; 3:10, 11).

The Choir and Congregational Singing

The choir consisted of at least twelve adult male singers. These singers were required to be of the Tribe of Levi, complete a five–year training period in music and worship, and dedicate themselves to full–time music ministry. They were to be set apart for service, sanctified with a clean heart, and between the ages of 35 and 50. They were paid for their services, provided housing, and treated as other religious workers without discrimination. While it was mandated choirs should be a minimum of 12 members, it was not at all uncommon for large, well–rehearsed choirs to lead in the celebration of great events and significant worship times. For example, Solomon's choir numbered 4,000 (1 Chron. 23:5), Zerubbabel's temple choir consisted of 200 singers (Ezra 2:65), and Nehemiah's temple choir included 245 men and women (Neh. 7:67).

A major portion of the musical performance involved the congregation singing Psalms in responsory style. Responsorial singing involved a leader singing a whole line, or the portion of a line, with the congregation answering with the second line of the verse.

Instrumental Music

The use of instruments by Hebrew musicians had an important place in the Old Testament. Instruments were regularly used to meet utilitarian demands rather than personal or social needs for self expression. The use of instruments was so important to the work of the ministry that when David organized the worship music for the temple he instructed the Levites to use instruments which he had personally made (1 Chron. 23:5b). A number of passages give details as to the construction and use of instruments in biblical worship. Some instruments, such as the tambourine, were not usually used in public worship because of their identity with heathen gods. Other instruments were reserved for special purposes such as weddings, mourning, warfare, and assembly. It is generally agreed the instruments mentioned in the Old Testament functioned in direct relationship with the life and routine of the Hebrew people and were associated with singers as a call to worship. These usages included: public ceremonies (Gen. 31:27), anointing of kings (1 Kings 1:39), in times of warfare (Judges 7:16–23), in the removal of the ark from Gibeah and then to Jerusalem (2 Sam. 6:5; 1 Chron. 15:28; 16:5), dedication of the second temple (Ezra 3:10), and the dedication of the wall of Jerusalem (Neh. 12:27).

Three families of instruments were used in praise to Jehovah: *stringed instruments, wind instruments,* and *percussion instruments. Stringed instruments* were used for sacred and secular purposes. They were especially popular in Hebrew worship. King David played stringed instruments. Instructions were given for specific psalms to be accompanied by stringed instruments; the lyre and harp were associated with the activities of prophetic bands. Tradition indicates nine or more lyres were always used in public worship.

John F. Wilson credited King David with discovering a technique common to modern acoustics and sound principles. Wilson wrote, "He discovered that the type of string, plus the tension with which it is attached, determines the pitch that will result. He also concluded that the shape and size of the frame that holds the strings determines the tone quality." Two principal types of stringed instruments were used: the harp and the psaltery. The harp (Hebrew *kinnor* pronounced *kin-nore'*), mentioned more frequently than any other Old Testament instrument, had broad appeal for use in the shepherd's field and King's court. The strings were plucked and the sound was amplified by a sound box at the base of the instrument, much like the modern–day guitar or lute. The psaltery (Hebrew *nevel* pronounced *nay'-bel*) or the ten–stringed instrument (Hebrew *'asor* pronounced *aw-sore'*) were used in the temple orchestra. The strings were strung across a curved neck, it lacked a finger board, and each string had one pitch.

Wind instruments included the pipes or organs, horns, and trumpets. The pipes (Hebrew *chalil* pronounced *khaw-leel'*, *neqeb* pronounced *neh'-keb*, and *muwtsaqah* pronounced *moo-saw-kaw'*) were tonal instruments with holes bored into the sides, allowing the musician to reproduce melody lines. In the Old Testament, the flutes (Hebrew *mashrowqiz* pronounced *mash-ro-kee'*) and the organ (*'ugav* pronounced *oo-gawb'*) were similar instruments. They were used for occasions of rejoicing, festival marching, dance accompaniment, and mourning for the dead.

Horns (Hebrew *shofar* pronounced *sho-far'*, *qeren* pronounced *keh'-ren*, or *yowbel* pronounced *yo-bale'*) were usually a hollowed–out ram's horn, restricted to a small number of pitches, with a mouth hole. It was used as an instrument to signal warfare, special festive days, and sacrifices. It is most commonly known as the instrument used to proclaim the year of Jubilee. The *shofar* is the only instrument presently used in the synagogue.

The trumpet (Hebrew *chatsotserah* pronounced *khats-o-tser-aw'*) was a straight tube made of silver and used for festivals, sacrifices, offerings, and to sound alarms in times of war. It was used in the coronation of a king and to herald worship of God. They were most often used in pairs, had no valves, and limited to only a few notes. According to John F. Wilson, "The historian Josephus believed that there were as many as two hundred thousand used in temple worship during the time of David and Solomon."

Five types of *percussion instruments* were used in the Old Testament. Cymbals (Hebrew *tslatsal* pronounced *tsel-aw-tsal'*) were constructed of copper or bronze and as the only percussion instruments permanently assigned to the temple, used in conjunction with stringed instruments for praise to Jehovah. The sistrum (Hebrew *mena'na'* pronounced *men-ah-ah'*), translated as "castenets" in 2 Samuel 6:5, was a shaker–like instrument, similar to the modern castanet and formed of metal. Bells (Hebrew *pa'amon* pronounced *pah-am-one'*), specifically referenced in Exodus 28:34, 35, were attached to the priest's robe so that "tinkling may be heard when he enters and leaves the holy place before the Lord, that he may not die." The timbrel or tabret (Hebrew *toph* pronounced *tofe*) was similar to the tambourine of today. It was a small hand–held instrument consisting of animal skins stretched over a cylindrical frame. It was usually played by women, beaten by hand and not used within the temple worship. The "musical instruments" in 1 Samuel 18:6 (Hebrew *shaliysh* pronounced *shaw-leesh'*) were probably like a modern triangle.

Banners and Dance

Reference to the use of banners and dance in the worship of Jehovah abound in the Old Testament. Banners (Hebrew *dagal* pronounced *daw-gal'*) and standards (Hebrew *degel* pronounced *deh'-gel* and *nec* pronounced *nace*) were used to represent ideals and aspirations, evoke emotions and devotion, and unify people under one purpose. There were three different purposes for banners and standards: to designate the location of a group (Num. 1:52; 2:2, 34), to be lifted up in the time of victory (Ps. 20:5), and as a rallying point for the congregation (Num. 21:8, 9). The banner marked the center of attention, place of hope, and center location for thanksgiving. God is referred to as Jehovah–Nissi or "my banner" in Exodus 17:15. A banner was erected as a call for soldiers to assemble in Isaiah 18 and the prophet Isaiah refers to the Messiah as a standard in Isaiah 49:22.

Dance was an important part of worship in ancient Israel. As the ark of the covenant was being moved into Jerusalem, "David was dancing before the Lord with all *his* might" (2 Sam. 6:14). There are three Hebrew words translated dance (*chuwl* pronouced *khool, raqad* pronounced *raw-kad'*, and *machowl* pronounced *maw-khole'*) that collectively appear 17 times (in the KJV). Lunde wrote, "One must be aware of the fact that dances were performed by men and women separately and void of sensuality" (*Christian Education Thru Music*, page 26).

To Sum It Up

Music in worship has always been a part of the human experience. It is a reflection of the daily life experience. Jubal is considered the father of all who make music. The use of music in the Old Testament included times of gathering harvest, war, merrymaking, feasting, and worship of God. The Book of Psalms is generally considered the Hebrew hymnal. King David organized music and worship with formal guidelines for the education, training, and employment of musicians for the House of God. Old Testament worship included choral and congregational singing, playing of instruments, and the presentation of banners and dance.

For Further Discussion

1. Imagine what it was like to be at the dedication of Solomon's Temple. Describe what you think you would have seen and heard. (Read 1 Kings 8,9; 2 Chronicles 5:1–7:10)
2. Review the Book of Psalms and find one psalm for each of the five types of psalms: Praise, History, Penitence, Imprecation and Messianic.
3. Do you think music is a gift from God, a human invention, or both? Why?
4. What are the different instruments which have been used in your church's worship services in the past year?

For Application

1. Choose a psalm and read it as a group in a responsorial style.
2. Create a design for a worship banner which would have complemented last Sunday's sermon at your church.
3. Write the music for a hymn using the text of a psalm as the lyrics.
4. How many songs in your church hymnal can you find which are based on an Old Testament text?

Survey of Music & Worship: New Testament Foundations

5

Our mind cannot conceive of God without
ascribing some worship to Him. —John Calvin

For some, it was an ordinary March day in 1978. For others, it was a day that would live in their memories forever. Family members stood around the bed where the lifeless body of Linda, a 32-year old wife, sister, and daughter lay; her eyes closed and lips forever silent. The hospital, with all its noise and dingy decor, only intensified the pain they felt on that March day. They stood, gazing at the stilled, silent face of one whose earthly life was gone forever. As the clock ticked away the afternoon moments, each family member quietly reflected on the beauty, joy, and fresh spirit that flowed freely from one they so dearly loved. The doctor had not yet arrived. Silent tears of sorrow flowed down their cheeks as the family held hands. They knew she was gone. Finally, after what seemed to be hours of silence, Linda's sister began singing:

There is a place of constant rest,
Near to the heart of God;
A place where sin cannot molest,
Near to the heart of God.
O Jesus, blest redeemer,
Sent from the heart of God,
Hold us that wait before Thee,
Near to the heart of God.
—*Near to the Heart of God* by Cleland B. McAfee

On that tragic, yet triumphant, afternoon, a family torn by the grief of death, experienced the presence of God.

Stories like Linda's effectively illustrate the differences between the Old Testament and New Testament approaches to music and worship. Old Testament worship primarily focused on Jehovah as Sovereign, Provider, and Redeemer. New Testament worship focuses on the expression of a personal relationship with Jehovah through His Son, Jesus Christ.

Music in the New Testament

References to music in the New Testament abound. Music was played (probably on the flute) at the time of a child's death (Matt. 9:23). There was music and dancing in Jesus' story of the prodigal son (Luke 15:25). Jesus and His disciples sang at the Last Supper (Matt. 26:30; Mark 14:26). There are a number of references that indicate the use of singing by Christians in worship (1 Cor. 14:15, 26; Eph. 5:19, 20; Col. 3:16; James 5:13). Paul and Silas sang in the Philippian prison (Acts 16:25). Christ is pictured as singing with the church (Heb. 2:12). A trumpet will sound to signal Christ's return for His Church (1 Thess. 4:16; 1 Cor. 15:52; Matt. 24:31). And heaven is described as being overflowing with music and worship. There, the angelic hosts are continuously praising God. John the Apostle pictures the elders and redeemed saints singing "new songs" of adoration to the Lord (Rev. 5:9–14; 14:1–3; 15:3, 4; 19:1–6).

Worship in the New Testament

The first description of worship in the New Testament is found in Acts 2:42, "And they were continually devoting themselves to the apostles' teaching and to fellowship, to the breaking of bread and to prayer."

The Church, born in the Holy flame of Pentecost, adopted a pattern of worship that is both similar to and yet distinct from Old Testament worship. In this verse, four elements of worship are described. Certainly these are not the only four elements in New Testament worship (there is no mention of music or baptism). But these four elements were certainly core to what the first Christians considered important. These elements were so important that they were "continually devoting themselves" to them.

First, the early church was committed to the teaching of the Apostles. The book of Acts begins with Peter's sermon in Jerusalem on the day of Pentecost and ends with Paul preaching to the Jews in Rome. Worship and the proclamation of the Word of God are inseparable. This does not mean that worship can only take place when someone is preaching or teaching. But it does mean that a vital part of the New Testament worship experience was the communication of God's Word and response to it.

Second, fellowship was a vital part of New Testament worship. The word translated fellowship is the Greek word *koinonia* (pronounced *koy-nohn-ee'-ah*). It means an intimate community. The same word occurs twice in 1 John 1:3, "What we have seen and heard we proclaim to you also, that you also may have fellowship with us; and indeed our fellowship is with the Father, and with His Son Jesus Christ."

According to John, fellowship is a three-way experience between God, John, and other believers. Although private worship is important, it is never to be a substitute for public, corporate worship. The fellowship of the New Testament church did not prevent them from experiencing difficulties, nor will it prevent us from doing so. But as we cultivate and strengthen our ties with fellow believers through shared worship experiences, we will be better prepared to face whatever circumstances we may encounter, no matter how difficult.

The third element in the passage is the "breaking of bread." While this term is the common phrase used for eating a meal, many commentators believe it is a reference to the Lord's Table. Jesus "broke bread" with His disciples in the upper room the night before His crucifixion, initiating a "new covenant" with them. This new covenant was sealed by the breaking of bread and the sharing of common cup of the fruit of the vine. The New Testament church regularly celebrated the Lord's Supper, perhaps in conjunction with a common meal. By participating in the Lord's Supper as part of worship, our attention is focused on the redemptive work of God through His Son Jesus for the remission of sin. In the Old Testament, believers offered sacrifices for their sins looking in faith to God for the provision of a covering for their sins. In the New Testament, believers still look in faith to God, thanking Him for the provision of salvation made possible through the sacrifice of Jesus.

The fourth element is prayer. The church was born in prayer, the church continued in prayer and when obstacles were encountered, the church won mighty victories in prayer. The entire book of Acts is testimony to the priority of prayer and its role in the life of the individual Christian and the Church.

Principles of Music in New Testament Worship

But what about the role of music in New Testament worship? While the New Testament does not give details as to the practice, style, or forms of music in the infant church, we can gain some insights from the study of Colossians 3:16, 17, along with its parallel passage in Ephesians 5:18–20. It is unfair to the text and to Paul to believe the church music program was primary in his mind as he wrote these words to the church at Colossae. Paul was more concerned with presenting Christ as the Head of the Church than he was with the principles of Christian music. But nestled between Paul's exhortation about holiness (v. 1–15) and his admonition to the family (v. 18–25) are two very practical verses that speak directly to the music and worship program in the church. In these verses there are four principles that, if applied, will help us produce a God-honoring music and worship ministry. The apostle wrote: "Let the word of Christ richly dwell within you, with all wisdom teaching and admonishing one another with psalms and hymns and spiritual songs, singing with thankfulness in your hearts to God. And whatever you do in word or deed, do all in the name of the Lord Jesus, giving thanks through Him to God the Father." (Col. 3:16, 17)

The Message of Music

Principle number one is the message of our music must be solidly based on the Word of God (Col. 3:16a). Paul emphasized musicians should be filled with an understanding of the Word of God and then communicate a biblically–based text through their music. The text of the music must contain a clear message from God's Word. God's Word must not only fill our hearts but must permeate the lyrics of the songs we use to worship Him as well. Thus, in evaluating music for use in the church, we must ask ourselves, "Is the text of this song consistent with biblical truth?"

Another important aspect of this principle involves the quality of God's Word in the musician, "richly dwell within you." "Dwell" means to inhabit or to become part of our being. It should be the controlling aspect of every Christian musician's disposition. The world teaches musicians to do their own thing, to strive to be "great musicians," to aspire for acceptance. But for the Christian, the Word of God is to serve as a regulator.

Several years ago I owned a small import automobile which served my young family well for several years. This car was so reliable, it seemed to repair itself! Then, during a hot summer day, I noticed the air conditioning cut off and on suddenly. I parked the car to go into a store. When I returned, the engine would not even turn over. A stranger helped me get the car started with the use of his jumper cables. Thinking the problem was the battery, I drove to a garage and purchased a new one. But on the way home the car was still having difficulty. My car sputtered back to the garage. This time they found the real problem—a faulty voltage regulator. I had the power (a new battery) and the right mode of transportation (my car). But the trip was rough because the voltage regulator was defective. So it is with music in the work of God. We can have the right melody, the right words, the right opportunity, a great sound track, and the emotion of the moment, but our ministry will be defective if we are not controlled by the spiritual "regulator," the Word of God.

The message of our music, the Word of God, is also to be evident in our lives "with all wisdom." This refers to our ability to discern between right and wrong, proper or improper, ethical and unethical in our selection and use of music. James promises us if we ask God for wisdom, we will receive it (James 1:5). The Christian musician needs the wisdom of God to know what song to use, how to perform it, and what innovations (if any) are appropriate in worship.

The Method of Music

The second principle is music should focus on the two-fold method of "teaching and admonishing one another" (Col. 3:16b). The word "teach" means to instruct, explain, and direct. Thus, music directed to God should be for more than entertainment or personal enjoyment. Music is to be used as a tool for biblical instruction and training. This is one of the reasons why music is so important to the ministry of Christian education. Just as the Bible can be taught through stories, audio–visual aids, small group activities, handcrafts, and many other methods, the Bible can also be taught effectively through music. Music should be more than just the prelude to the Bible lesson or sermon. The right kind of music can be used powerfully to teach the truths of God's Word! Many of the great hymn writers such as Martin Luther, Isaac Watts, and the Wesley brothers, realized the power of music to teach and wrote hymns rich in doctrinal truths. Music can also be used to help people memorize the very words of Scripture. Many children and adults who have difficulty memorizing Bible verses can usually learn the words to a song much easier.

"Admonish" means to invite, encourage, shape, and mold. A scriptural music ministry provides opportunity for musicians to encourage, build up, and spiritually nurture fellow believers. Christian musicians have a responsibility to teach and to train people to understand and perform God's work.

The focus of the musician's efforts in teaching and admonishing is "one another." This means the music ministry is not exclusive to any one group of individuals. To be scriptural, the ministry must include all of God's people. All believers are to be involved in the ministry of music regardless of their musical skill. God desires for us to minister to Him and to one another with our sacrifices of music. No one is to be merely a spectator in the music program of the local church.

The Music for the Musician

The third principle of a New Testament music ministry involves the music itself. Paul instructs us to use "psalms and hymns and spiritual songs." "Psalms" and "hymns" are spiritual odes or melodies, essentially one in the same. These are melodies with words based on Scripture passages, doctrinal truths or biblical principles. They include, but are not limited to, songs about God, to God, and because of God. In making application to our churches today, "psalms" may include any melody with a text based on Scripture while "hymns" are songs that teach dogma or doctrine.

"Spiritual songs" probably refer to any song used in the church sung in the power of the Holy Spirit designed to meet spiritual needs. Today the word "spiritual" may refer to the style, sound, and sometimes cultural identity of a composition. But this is not what Paul had in mind. The key word in the phrase is "spiritual." It is significant to note the only other occurrence of this phrase is located in Ephesians 5:19, a parallel passage. The context of Ephesians 5 is Paul's admonition to the church to be "filled with the Spirit" (Eph. 5:18). Thus, "spiritual songs" refer to songs sung under the control of the Holy Spirit as well as songs which meet spiritual needs within the congregation. A strong implication is that believers should make a conscious effort to avoid performing music that speaks only to the flesh, our non–spiritual natures.

The Motive of the Musician

The fourth principle is the musician must have the proper motives in their music. "Singing with thankfulness in your hearts to God. And whatever you do in word or deed, do all in the name of the Lord Jesus, giving thanks through Him to God the Father" (v. 16d, 17).

"Singing with thankfulness" has to do with our attitude. This attitude should include a sense of gratitude to God for all He has done for us and the desire to bring glory to Him through every aspect of lives—including music. As we are singing, we are to focus our attention on God, the giver of "every good gift and every perfect gift" (James 1:17 KJV). God does not need us to sing in order to hear music. He has the angels. But God is more concerned about why we are singing to Him than the fact we are singing to Him. Misguided motives and selfish ambitions have hindered many gifted musicians from communicating the gospel of Jesus Christ. There is no room in the service of God for musicians with arrogant, self–righteous, condescending, or self–serving attitudes.

"Singing . . . in your hearts" refers to the source of the song. For our music and worship to be acceptable to God, it must begin in our hearts. God is more concerned about the music in our hearts than He is with the music on our lips. God is in the business of changing hearts—molding, strengthening, developing, and sanctifying them for His glory. Music is a means for communicating outwardly what God is doing inwardly.

One final area related to the musician's motive is detailed in verse 16, "singing . . . to God." Paul places this phrase after a section dealing with Christian living and before a verse commanding us to give God the glory in everything. Singing to the Lord implies at least three things for the Christian musician.

First, Christian musicians have the responsibility to present God their very best—at all times. He deserves no less. Every aspect of our practice of music and worship should exemplify appreciation and praise for who God is and what He is doing in our lives. Musicians should present to God gifts which are excellent. In part, this will mean a commitment to invest the resources necessary to develop the musical gifts of those who are part of the body of Christ. However, we should not aim for excellence for the sake of excellence or drawing attention to our own gifts but to bring praise to a God who rules the universe.

Second, musicians have the responsibility to minister *to* God. While we may often communicate to one another, our first responsibility is to sing to God. As we minister to God through our music, He will in turn minister to us. Thus, our primary focus in worship should not be on what we can get out of the experience but rather what we can give to God through the experience.

Third, our motives in presenting music should be to glorify God, not to earn the approval of others. Many a well–intended minister of music, music group, soloist, or instrumentalist has been fooled by Satan into thinking that God is impressed with abilities, talents, technology, and ego and that He will bless us according to the level of the compliments we receive on our performance. While God certainly can use our abilities for His glory, He does not have to have them. Our abilities in music are gifts God has loaned us to use for the purpose of glorifying Him. To paraphrase an old saying, "The musical talents you possess are God's gifts to you. How you develop and use those musical talents are your gifts to God."

Questions to Ask When Selecting Music for Worship

Colossians 3:16, 17 serves as a basis for the following questions you should ask as you select music (both instrumental and vocal) for use in worship.

1) Are the lyrics of the composition consistent with the biblical truth?
2) Does the composition teach doctrinal truths and/or biblical principles?
3) Does the composition admonish (warn and encourage)?
4) Does the composition utilize the words of Scripture (a psalm), focus attention on God (a hymn), or emphasize what God is doing in the life of a spirit–filled believer (a spiritual song)?

5) Does the composition call more attention to its musical style or form of presentation than the lyrics or the melody?
6) Does the composition cause those who play it, sing it, and listen to it to have an inward spirit of thankfulness toward God?

To Sum It Up

Old Testament worship primarily focused on the presentation of Jehovah as Sovereign. New Testament worship was an expression of a personal relationship with Jehovah through His Son, Jesus Christ. The New Testament abounds with references to the use of music in church worship. Acts 2:42 gives us a pattern of New Testament worship. Colossians 3:16, 17 provides four principles which can guide us in the selection and use of music in worship. The message of our music must be solidly based on the Word of God. The method of our music should focus on teaching and building up the Body of Christ through the music program of the local church. Music in the church should conform to the pattern established by the Apostle Paul in Colossians chapter three: psalms, hymns, and spiritual songs. We must work hard to maintain the proper motive in the music program. This passage also provides six questions that should be asked when selecting music for use in worship.

For Further Discussion

1. What are some of the differences between Old Testament and New Testament approaches to music and worship?
2. What are principles of music in the church that can be found in the following passages: 1 Corinthians 14:15, 26; Ephesians 5:19, 20; James 5:13?
3. What are some of the improper motives which can be present in a music ministry? How can these be prevented or overcome?

For Application

1. At random, pick out 10–15 hymns from your church's current hymnal. Identify which are "psalms and hymns" and which are "spiritual songs."
2. In a small group of three to five, try your hand at writing the words to a "hymn" and then a "spiritual song."
3. For the next four weeks, check the balance between "psalms and hymns" and "spiritual songs" used in your church's worship services. Can you find a pattern?

Survey of Music & Worship: A.D. 300 to 19th Century England

6

I have no pleasure in any man who despises music. It is no invention of ours; it is the gift of God. I place it next to theology.
—Martin Luther

About A.D. 110, the Roman Emperor Trajan wrote to Pliny the Younger, who was serving as governor of Bithynia. Trajan was inquiring of Pliny as to what was behind the spread of the Christian faith throughout the empire. Pliny investigated and sent this reply to Trajan, "They are accustomed to meet on a fixed day before daylight to sing a hymn of praise to Christ as God."

Perhaps Pliny did not understand the motivation for their worship, but he could easily see the results of their worship. As Christians worshiped Jesus Christ as God through their singing, their preaching, their fellowship, and their celebration of the Lord's Table, God moved throughout the Roman Empire in bringing thousands to know the joy of salvation and the privilege of worship.

In the early church, emphasis was given to what was in the heart of the believer and not the location where the Christians would meet for music and worship. For the most part, the early church was a loosely–structured organization and in many places, it was primarily an underground group. Many believers were in mortal danger because of their commitment to Christ. Thus, they were not primarily concerned with the beauty of a building in which to meet, the structure of a service, or the importance of a particular worship tradition to uphold. But they were interested in worship!

These early believers gave more attention to the ministry of encouragement, instruction, comfort, and edification than to establishing guidelines for liturgy. Their purpose in music and worship was to focus on communicating to one another a vital, personal relationship with Jesus Christ.

As the church spread throughout the Roman Empire during the first three centuries after Pentecost, the persecution of believers increased, and thus the church made limited use of public singing, primarily due to governmental persecution. Meetings for praise and fellowship were often held in secret. Consequently, many of the early Christians hymns focused on the message of the gospel and praising the risen Christ.

Music in the Church Prior to the Reformation (A.D. 300–1500)

In spite of persecution, the church continued to grow in its first three centuries. Following A.D. 313, Christianity was proclaimed the official religion of the Roman Empire and singing by Christian congregations became more expressive. By the fourth century A.D., distinctions began to be drawn between clergy and laity. The church became a powerful political system of patriarchs, priests, bishops, and deacons. No longer were the clergy servants and representatives of their congregations. The clergy in the Roman Catholic Church saw themselves as exclusive channels through which divine grace was transmitted to the faithful. In this position, the clergy assumed the responsibility for forming and shaping the liturgy, selecting and performing music for worship, and directing all worship activities.

Five basic types of hymn writing were developed from A.D. 300 to 1500. The first four were the result of the clergy and the fifth was an outgrowth of personal expression by laity. The forms were:

1) *Ambrosian Hymnody.* This was characterized by three forms of hymn singing: responsorial psalm singing, antiphonal psalm singing and the metrical hymn.

2) *Office Hymns.* This type was an adaptation of Latin hymns for use in daily worship in monasteries.

3) *The Gregorian Chant.* By the end of the seventh century, the melodies of the Roman chant were officially recognized by the Church. Named after Pope Gregory I, these chants were characterized as monophonic (one melody line with little or no harmony), unaccompanied, diatonic (not usually changing keys), without strict meter, and had the rhythmic freedom to match a chosen text. The melodies associated with Gregorian Chants were widely used and accepted by clergy and laity alike. Recent recordings of Gregorian Chants have become best–sellers, demonstrating their continued strong appeal.

4) *Early Latin Hymns.* The Roman Catholic Church maintained that all worship had to be conducted in Latin by the clergy. Thus, the songs associated with Ambrosian hymnody were written to be sung in Latin. Hymn singing by the clergy gradually became a part of local church worship services which was accepted universally by the Roman Catholic Church by the twelfth century.

5) *Laudi Spirituali*. By the thirteenth and fourteenth centuries a body of non–liturgical music developed in Italy outside the auspices of the Roman Catholic Church. Called *laudi spirituali*, these songs were religious songs of devotion and praise to God, set to simple, secular–like melodies, in the common vernacular of the people. These songs were highly popular but never used in official worship services.

The Protestant Reformation

Protestant worship and congregational singing, as we know it today, began with the Protestant Reformation. From the time of the Laodicean Council in the fourth century until the sixteenth century, the Roman Catholic Church had almost succeeded in completely eliminating congregational singing from worship services. Congregrants were spectators rather than participants in worship. This lack of lay involvement in worship services was one of the many factors which led to what we call now the Protestant Reformation. A dominant leader in the Reformation was the German priest, Martin Luther. The beginning of the Reformation is traced to October 31, 1517, when Luther publicly expressed his criticisms of the practices of the Roman Catholic Church he felt were unscriptural and corrupt.

Luther had a passion for communicating the Word of God to the people so they could understand it. He translated the Bible into his native German from the Greek and Hebrew. He not only wanted the people to read God's Word in their own language but to have the opportunity to sing in their own language as well.

Two basic musical forms flowed out of the Reformation Movement:

1) *The German Chorale*. Luther reinstituted the importance of congregational singing as an integral part of public worship with what eventually became known as the German Chorale. This style of music was written in four parts with the melody in the soprano voice and was harmonized with simple chords. This resulted in a revival of hymn singing in churches with the congregation participating in simple four–part harmony. Luther believed God spoke to His people through the Scriptures and they in turn responded to God through their hymns. He used congregational singing to encourage lay participation in worship as well as to communicate doctrine and theology in the vernacular.

Luther himself wrote scores of hymns but today only about ten are used in English–speaking churches. Luther's most famous hymn, *A Mighty Fortress is Our God*, is a paraphrase of Psalm 46.

2) *The Metrical Psalm*. John Calvin was a leader of the Reformation in Switzerland. It was his conviction that congregational singing should be from the Psalms of the Old Testament. He recognized

the value of singing to nourish holy living and worship. Calvin felt that since music was for everyone, it needed to be simple. And, since it was used to express worship to a sovereign God, it needed to be modest. These two qualities were achieved by unaccompanied (a capella) singing and the exclusive use of the Psalms as source material for all public and private worship music.

The metrical structure of the psalms followed the pattern of the popular songs of the day. William Reynolds describes the Metrical Psalms as songs "inherited from the trouvères and troubadours of previous centuries." These hymns included the singing in unison of four or more lines from the Psalms.

The Publication of Psalters

The invention of the printing press not only increased the distribution of Bibles but that of hymnals as well. One of the most important contributions of this period was seen in the publication of *The Genevan Psalter* (1562). This Psalter was a collection of tunes to be used with selections from the book of Psalms. It was a monumental publication that impacted the church worship for many years: "In the following 38 years, more than 80 other editions were published, and during 1600–1685, at least ninety more editions were published. From Geneva, the *Genevan Psalter* spread through France and on throughout Christendom. Perhaps no other publication has so influenced Christian song." (Reynolds, p. 33)

Psalters began to be created and used throughout the Christian world. John Hopkins and Thomas Sternhold constructed a publication called *The Whole Book of Psalms* (1563). In England, John Knox was influential in helping to create *The Anglo–Genevan Psalter* (1558) and *The Scottish Psalter* (1564) in Scotland. *The Ainsworth Psalter* (1592) was compiled by Christians in Holland. Matthew Parker, Archbishop of Canterbury, published a hymnbook in 1560. William Damon published *The Psalter* (1579) in London. Thomas Este's *Psalter* (1592) was the first to provide four–part harmony for all the tunes. *The Genevan Psalter, The Whole Book of Psalms* and *The Ainsworth Psalter* were used by Christians seeking religious freedom in the Massachusetts Colony in the 1620s and 1630s.

An important part of German hymn singing which co-existed with the Lutheran chorale tradition was Moravian Hymnody. The Moravians, also known as the Bohemian Brethren, were followers of John Hus of Bohemia and practiced congregational singing as early as the late fifteenth century. Their first collection of 89 hymns, published in Europe, predated both Luther and Calvin.

Western European Hymnody (A.D. 1600 to 1900)

Congregational singing in England was actually initiated by the Particular (Calvinistic) Baptist churches sometime between 1671 and 1685. Psalm singing was the dominant expression of congregational music throughout Great Britain. The transition from Psalms to hymns was slow and met with strong resistance by the Anglicans and Presbyterians. The move from strict use of Metrical Psalms to hymns was often a progression from the literal singing of a psalm text to a free paraphrasing of the Psalms. This development continued as gradually other scripture passages were used for hymn texts and then resulted in what were called *Hymns of Human Composure*. These hymns were based on devotional material and were first used for family devotions. It was gradually introduced into the church for special services such as the celebration of the Lord's Supper, and then finally was freely used in public worship.

A new epoch of congregational singing began with the hymns of Isaac Watts. Called by many the "Father of English Hymnody," Watts believed the song of the New Testament church should express the gospel of the New Testament, regardless of the musical or literary form. He composed hymns which were expressions of praise and devotion based on his own experience. Watts taught that songs should express the thoughts and feelings of those who sang rather than relate the experiences and circumstances of the Psalm writers. Watts often used hymns to teach Calvinistic theology and summarize his sermons.

John and Charles Wesley were also important contributors to English Hymnody. The Wesley brothers were known on both sides of the Atlantic for their participation in the time of great revival known today as the Great Awakening. Together they wrote and translated more than 6,500 hymns. They used hymns to propagate Methodist theology which was often strongly opposed to the Calvinism of Watts. They were both very concerned about the manner in which congregations sang and strongly held to the practice of singing without instruments.

Other hymn writers and publishers of songs for the evangelical churches in England included John Rippon, John Newton, William Cowper, Philip Dodderidge, William Williams, and George Whitefield. With strong biblical preaching and hearty hymn singing as their guide, these men helped to lead England into a nineteenth century revival that spread to America and stimulated changes in worship practices still observed today.

Hymn writers of the seventeenth and eighteenth century were concerned with composing hymns that expressed both doctrine and personal conviction. During the nineteenth century, hymn writers were influenced by a renewed interest in the classics. They were often more interested in intellectual and creative fulfillment than in the emotional expression of theological tenets.

A new religious movement known as the Oxford or Tractarian Movement began in England during the 1830s. The Oxford emphasis was a reaction to the many indifferent and careless worship services conducted by the more independent and non–conformist congregations. The Oxford Movement produced an important hymnal known as *Hymns Ancient and Modern*. Published in England in 1837, this book became a major reference resource on hymnody. Selections were carefully chosen with songs of evangelical origin omitted altogether.

Hymns written following the Oxford Movement are generally classified as part of the Victorian Era with several categories:

1) *High Church Hymns*. The writers of these hymns were Anglicans who resisted what they saw as a drift toward Rome. They were concerned with preserving the integrity of liturgical practices and traditions of the day.

2) *Evangelical* or *Low Church Hymns*. These writers were characterized by a concern for the spiritual and social welfare of individuals.

3) *Broad Church Hymns*. These hymns were written by those who represented the liberal and modern factions in the Anglican Church.

4) *Dissenting Hymns*. These writers were in congregations (such as Presbyterian, Methodist and Baptist churches) that had broken from the established state churches in England. Hymn singing reached a new level of spiritual vitality during this period of time.

5) *Post–Victorian Hymns*. The Post–Victorian Church hymn writers wrote after the death of Queen Victoria in 1901. Their hymns were a reaction against what they felt to be literary and musical triteness represented in the writing of earlier Oxford and Victorian artists.

To Sum It Up

The New Testament philosophy of music is a spiritual rather than secular approach. The New Testament focused on music as a form of communication to others of a vital, personal relationship with Jesus Christ. By the sixteenth century, the Roman Catholic Church had almost eliminated congregational singing. The Protestant Reformation, led by men such as Luther and Calvin, brought back congregational singing in the language of the people. English hymnody made great contributions to church music through the ministries of Isaac Watts, the Wesley brothers, and others. In England during the seventeenth to nineteenth centuries, hymn writing was subdivided into a number of categories. Many of these hymns continue to be used throughout the Church today.

For Further Discussion

1. How would persecution affect the church and its worship practices today?
2. Why do you believe the Roman Catholic Church promoted the division between clergy and laity? Do you believe this could happen today? Why or why not?
3. What are the benefits of congregational singing?

For Application

1. Using your church's hymnal, look for the oldest hymns. Note the name of the writer, where the writer lived, and in which of the categories (listed in this chapter) the writer fits.
2. Look in your church's hymnal to find hymns which teach the following doctrines: the virgin birth of Christ, the resurrection of Christ, the blood atonement, the inspiration of Scripture, the second coming of Christ, the importance of prayer, faith as a condition of salvation.
3. Select one hymn by Isaac Watts and one hymn by Charles Wesley from your church's hymnal. What are the similarities and the differences of the two hymns?

Survey of Music & Worship: 1800 to the Present

7

Music was as vital as the church edifice itself, more deeply stirring than all the glory of glass or stone. Many a stoic soul, doubtful of the creed, was melted by the music, and fell on his knees before the mystery that no words can speak. —Will Durant

The two Great Awakenings stimulated change in the application and presentation of music and worship. The expression of a personal relationship with God became more public. A renewed emphasis on evangelism provided opportunity for music to be used as a platform for presenting the gospel. As with the early Church, the purpose for music and worship was to honor, adore, exalt, and magnify God. But the focus of Christian music in the ninteenth century and into the twenty–first century was on the intentional adaptation of popular musical styles for use in and by the Church. As the Church grew across Europe and into the Americas, music and worship forms continued to develop.

Overview of Evangelical Music in America (1800–1930)

In North America, all gospel music genres trace their heritage to the pre–eighteenth century singing schools where "lining out the phrase" (the music director singing a line and the congregation singing the line after him) and oral traditions were accepted methods of music education in the church. Prior to 1800, almost all American congregations used Watts, the Wesleys, and other European hymn writers as source material for their worship services.

By 1800, the folk music style of camp meetings in America was combined with texts that expressed a personal faith in God and encouraged congregational singing. This combination created a popular sacred style that was a precursor of the gospel song. The Camp Meeting movement of 1800 is remembered particularly for its spontaneous, improvised music based on secular folk idioms.

Changes in Music

Around 1820, a division between northern and southern American traditions in musical instruction affected the development of music in the North American evangelical church. The sheer number of migrants moving to the United States after 1790 challenged music publishers to change their practices. These European migrants brought with them a rounded–note notational practice and a hymn tradition based on slower harmonic rhythm, parallel thirds and sixths, and the more common major keys. This tradition, called *The Reformed Branch* (or *Progressive Movement*), encouraged music instruction and aided in the establishment of church and public school music, music conventions, choral societies and festivals, summer music schools, music normal institutes, and the publication of all types of music. *The Reformed Branch*, inspired by city revivalism, secular folk music, and Sunday school songs, was accepted in the northern states.

In contrast, the South was more conservative and gave preference to maintaining the traditions taught by the old eighteenth century singing school movement. Known as *The Character Notation Group*, it used unique pedagogical methodologies and varied approaches to music notation. This group continued their singing school tradition and published oblong–shaped note tune books.

From the 1840s on, a new body of songs were adapted by the American Sunday school. Large citywide revivals, led by such notables as Charles Finley, gave opportunity to present camp meeting and other "folk" songs to the public. Throughout the first half of the nineteenth century, the influence of secular folk music on the evangelical music culture increased and the time needed to adapt these styles for sacred music use decreased. By 1850, sacred music composers were able to adapt and incorporate secular musical styles of the preceding generation, but remained hesitant to compose in their own generation's secular musical styles. Only after a particular form, genre, or style became respectable within society's musical culture, could individuals of a later generation accept it as appropriate for religious expression.

The popular Sunday school movement provided a platform for the presentation of new songs promoting evangelical theology to children. By 1870, Ira Sankey, a famous composer and companion to evangelist Dwight L. Moody, coined the term "gospel music." Sankey popularized the singing of gospel texts set to "secular" tunes. During the years of 1850 to 1910, three sub–genres of gospel music evolved for use in the evangelical community. They were *Traditional Gospel Music*, *Southern Gospel Music*, and *Black Gospel Music*.

Traditional Gospel Music

Sometimes referred to as the "northern gospel song," this style was essentially patterned after the German art song. A stanza, communicating an important gospel textual thought, is followed by a chorus or refrain that drives home the message in summary (Mel Wilhoit, 1991, p. 13). Less emphasis was placed on rhythm. Two types of songs characterized traditional gospel music prior to 1900: the gospel song and its derivative, the gospel hymn.

The gospel song found its origin in the Sunday school movement of the citywide revivals of the 1850s. In contrast, the gospel hymn, "came forth as a major force in urban revivalism" (Eskew and McElrath, 1980, pp. 177, 178) in the 1870s. It was musically more sophisticated, theologically more conservative, and often expressed an intimate relationship and commitment to God.

Southern Gospel or Singing Convention Style

Southern Gospel style is most commonly characterized by the gospel male quartet and music in the fa–sol–la singing school tradition, sometimes called Singing Convention Style. In contrast to traditional gospel music, Southern Gospel music, or as some refer to it as "shaped–note gospel" hymnody, was usually a rural or small-town phenomenon.

There were two approaches to performing and ministry for those singing Southern Gospel. The first was the Southern Gospel singing school style. For better than 100 years (1850–1960), congregational singing was of premier importance in the South. The singing school was a social, educational, and religious event in rural, southern communities. Singing from shaped–note books developed into a tradition for southern evangelicals. Through the 1960s, the singing school, with the singing school master, was an important method of music education in the South. Singing schools were usually held for one- or two–week periods at a local church. Monthly "class singing" sometimes grew out of these singing schools. Publishers produced little softback songbooks for the purpose of "class singing."

The second approach to singing identified as Southern Gospel music involved singing conventions. The singing convention was different from the singing school. It usually a one- or two–day meeting. There representatives from publishing companies promoted their song books and were often presented as special performing artists.

Black Gospel

Singers of traditional Black Gospel have most closely followed the African concept of using a *Griot* as a soloist, preacher, and/or song leader. *Griot* is a French word commonly used to describe the ceremonial role that an African leader has in stimulating audience participation through spoken word, song, or drama. Depending upon their location, African–American congregations adapted their oral traditions to both the northern revival song practices and southern shaped–note singing. The literature was the same as that of pre-dominantly white congregations but the method of singing was entirely African–American.

Modern African–American religious music is referred to as *Black Gospel* and characterized by spontaneous solos and improvised vocal counterpoint. Black Gospel music is often highly rhythmic and usually taught as part of an oral tradition. Black Gospel music, in its early years, simply mirrored music of the great revivals experienced by the evangelical population in general.

While Black Gospel music maintained its unique presentation, Sankey's gospel hymns, Sunday school songs, and the Watts hymns remained popular with African–American congregations. However, during the years of 1900–1930, a Black Gospel music genre emerged. Stylistically, it was influenced by the spiritual, jazz, rhythm and blues, and singing associated with the Pentecostal Holiness tradition. Its theological and musical beginnings were traced to the Azusa Street Revival which occurred in Los Angeles between 1906 and 1909. The music was based on the gospel song tradition of Ira Sankey and Philip Bliss and performed with hand–clapping, bodily movement, shouts, and ornamentation of the melody. African–Americans made up a large part of the Azusa Street Revival movement's new followers and encouraged a style of church music that allowed expression of personal feelings and experience (Mel Wilhoit, 1991, p. 14). The beginnings of African–American gospel song coincided with the origin of ragtime, blues, and jazz.

Impact of Dynamic Individuals on Gospel Music (1800–1930)

One can safely say gospel music moved forward in direct relationship to the influence of particular song leaders who were famous in their time. These talented evangelical musicians promoted and distributed new music to evangelical churches and denominations.

The music of hymn writers such as Lowell Mason, Thomas Hastings, Joshua Leavitt, George Root, William Bradbury, and Robert Lowry helped propel great city revivals in the 1820s and 1830s. Secular folk music composers such as Stephen Foster and Dan Emmett served as models for these evangelical song writers. Composers such as Philip Bliss, William Doane, William Bradbury, George Root, Ira Sankey, and Ralph Hudson composed in this form, using the heightened emotional lyrics that distance gospel hymns from most traditional Protestant hymns.

As the first music supervisor of Boston City public schools and founder of the Boston Music Academy, Lowell Mason was better known as a publisher of music and pioneer in American music education than composer of Sunday school songs. He did, however, influence a number of talented evangelical musicians to publish and write in the fledgling, new gospel style. One composer deeply influenced by Mason was William Bradbury, a graduate of the Boston Academy of Music, writer of gospel songs, and composer of tunes for the famous blind gospel hymn writer Fanny Crosby. Bradbury's most famous tune is the familiar setting of *Jesus Loves Me*.

George Stebbins credits Ira Sankey with coining the term "gospel hymns." Ira Sankey was born in Edinburgh, Pennsylvania, on August 28, 1840, and received his formal musical instruction at a series of 12–week music conventions in Farmingtown, Ohio, led by Lowell Mason associates Will Bradbury, George F. Root, and George Webb. He joined Dwight L. Moody, a well–known evangelist from Chicago, in early 1887 to become one of the first preacher–singer teams. Sankey compiled 16 different song book collections. His *Gospel Songs and Solos* (1881) sold over 70 million copies by the end of 1934 and more than 90 million copies by 1961.

Homer A. Rodeheaver joined noted evangelist Billy Sunday in 1910 and was famous for leading enthusiastic congregational singing and large choirs (often numbering in the thousands of voices). The choir was a spectacle itself and an integral part of each service, singing a wide range of music. By the end of Rodeheaver's career, he was credited with a large number of copyrighted holdings including *The Old Rugged Cross* and *In the Garden*.

Thomas A. Dorsey contributed to gospel music in general and Black Gospel music in particular. The inclusion of hand clapping, percussion instruments, vamping via repeated chord progressions over which the soloist improvises, and the sixteen–bar blues form contributed to the style so readily identified with Dorsey's music. Dorsey used a previously existing oral tradition, the melodic and harmonic patterns of the blues, and his experience as a blues/jazz pianist to establish a genre of music easily accessible to singers that clearly presented the gospel.

Overview of Evangelical Music in America from 1930–1970

Growth experienced by evangelical churches following World War II prompted the establishment of many parachurch organizations. Newly founded Bible colleges trained music ministers, who, in turn, promoted and developed a new gospel choral tradition. Three movements, identified with various personalities, influenced the development of gospel music: the mass evangelistic campaigns, the advent of radio, and the youth movement. The Billy Graham Crusades helped promote new gospel music through the efforts of music director Cliff Barrows and soloist George Beverly Shea. *The Old–Fashioned Revival Hour* and other radio ministries provided a platform for the presentation of new music through choirs, quartets, and small ensembles.

More and more changes in church music were tied to changes within culture. For example, the unprecedented growth of Southern and Black Gospel music during the 1930s to 1970s may be attributed to demographic shifts. Evangelicals who moved from rural communities in Tennessee, Kentucky, western North Carolina, Alabama, and Georgia to the cities of the industrial North, took their cultural and religious practices with them.

There were several prominent composers of gospel music from 1940 to 1970. Among them was John W. Peterson who set the stage for future development of gospel music by creating new gospel songs based on secular musical styles. Peterson's major contribution was in creating the gospel cantata as a new choral genre.

Another composer of this time was Ralph Carmichael. He established a standard of excellence by recording gospel music with technical, musical, and artistic quality equal to any secular record label. He merged the sounds created in the Hollywood studios with evangelical lyrics and the excitement and energy of the youth music of the 1960s and 1970s.

Southern and Black Gospel music from 1940–1970 grew out of similar secular ethnic, cultural, and religious influences. Southern Gospel music developed through singing conventions and Southern Gospel quartet venues. Softback songbooks and sheet music with shaped–note engravings were printed by and used in publishing company–sponsored singing schools and conventions. The Southern Gospel quartet popularized new compositions through radio and concerts.

Gospel music for the African–American evangelical was primarily an oral tradition. Jubilee quartets and singing groups helped popularize the gospel song through recordings and radio. Thomas Dorsey and few other arrangers and composers of Black Gospel music secured copyright holdings to their songs and sold sheet music at concerts, from their automobiles, in churches, and at special concerts. Writers of Southern Gospel music were influenced by the jazz harmonies, rhythms, and songs of African–American musicians.

While some evangelical churches developed new forms of musical expression, other churches, mostly of Anglican heritage, experienced renewal of sacred classical compositions. By the end of the century, there emerged a distinct difference in music for the evangelical community and music for this more traditional church. Congregations identifying with traditional worship often feature classical literature with an emphasis on the liturgical church year. Publications from G. Schirmer, E. C. Schirmer, Beckenhorst Music, Hope Publishing, The Lorenz Company, Abingdon Press, Church Street Music, Shawnee Press, Augsburg Music, and Hinshaw Music feature popular composers from England and Canada such as Brian Jeffry Leech, Brian Wren, David Wilcox, John Rutter, and William Mathias. Prominent American composers writing in this tradition include: John Ness Beck, Gordon Young, Alan Pote, Bob Burroughs, Gregg Sewell, John Carter, Alice Parker, Gilbert Martin, and Mark Hayes. Much like southern gospel music, music of this genre was popularized by solo artists, singing groups, and ensembles with two prominent ensembles being the Robert Shaw Chorale and the St. Olaf Choir.

The Influences and Changes of the 1960s and 1970s

During the late 1960s and early 1970s an evangelical spiritual revival emerged out of the counter–cultural American Hippie movement. Dubbed by the media "The Jesus Movement," teenagers and young adults across America and western Europe turned to Christ for salvation. The West coast became a focal point of concentrated activity. Thousands of young people joined outreach teams, youth Bible studies, beach ministries, witness teams, Christian communes, and halfway house ministries. Music groups, employing conventional pop instrumentation of the time, were organized for evangelization and the nurture of new believers.

Two significant contributions are traced to the Jesus Movement: contemporary Christian music (CCM) and Scripture songs and choruses. Contemporary Christian music is music based on popular forms, sounds, rhythms, melodies, instrumentation, and culture with distinctly evangelical lyrics. Early contemporary artists were Keith Green and Steve Camp.

The Influences and Changes Since 1980

More recent times have seen the popularization of Scripture songs. Scripture songs, which are easy–to–sing choruses, are also called "Praise and Worship songs." These simple verses with a refrain, written for congregational use, are often based on a direct quotation or paraphrase of Scripture.

In the beginning, Scripture songs and choruses were primarily used by youth choirs and home Bible study groups. Evangelical congregations used these songs to musically reflect a personal encounter with Jesus Christ, renewing enthusiasm for congregational singing.

Scores of new, innovative music publishing companies rushed to meet the demands of this new "Praise and Worship Movement." New hymnals and music publications, with support media of all kinds, flooded the market. Ministers of music and worship leaders integrated multi-media, Powerpoint™ presentations, drama, and music into one package for the worship service. Using praise and worship as a platform for communication, musicians and worship pastors adapted pop styles, harmonies, and rhythms to religious texts and created a new form called contemporary worship. Propelled by the rapid growth in technology and communication media, many North American congregations abandoned their hymnals in preference to overhead and video projectors (lyrics on a screen), small rhythm bands, and three to six member ensembles, called praise teams. Many ministers of music discarded the organ for electronic keyboard and disbanded the choir in preference to praise and worship teams.

By the turn of the century, evangelical music practices often identified themselves with 1) Traditional Worship (structured and conservative, primarily using hymns and gospel songs); 2) Contemporary Worship (somewhat less structured and progressive in musical taste, often with innovative and newly written material and heavily incorporating multi-media and drama); and 3) Blended Worship (structured but flexible and cautiously eclectic with respect to the strategic blending of old and new worship elements).

To Sum It Up

From 1750 into the 21st century, the use of popular music styles with theologically conservative gospel texts used music of the common vernacular to communicate truth. The early Christians expressed a personal and vital relationship with the Lord. Perhaps it may be said that Christian music today, with its broad, eclectic appeal and stylistic sophistication is no less sincere than the worship of our early Christian brothers and sisters 2,000 years ago.

For Further Discussion

1. Where does your church fit into the history of church music described in this chapter?
2. Find an older member of your congregation who recalls the singing schools of the early twentieth century. Ask that person to share with the group a first-person description of a singing school.

3. Ask a person who has lived in different parts of the country to describe the differences (if any) between church musical styles from region to region.

For Application

1. Find the oldest hymnal in your congregation (you may need to ask your pastor or music pastor). As you examine it, what are the similarities and differences between this hymnal and the one your church currently uses?
2. Build a worship service around singing one song which was written in each of the following historical periods: 1830–1900; 1901–1930; 1931–1970; 1971–1990; 1991 to the present.
3. Take a verse or short passage from the New Testament and write the music so your group can sing it as a "Praise and Worship" song.

Principles for Renewing
Music & Worship – Part 1

8

There is more said in the Bible about praise than prayer, and music and song have not only accompanied all Scriptural revivals, but are essential in deepening spiritual life. —D. L. Moody

It was the second Sunday of a four–year tenure in what proved to be the most fulfilling church in my career as a minister of music. I stepped up to the platform and began leading the congregation in singing *Brethren, We Have Met to Worship* a capella. The pastor nodded approvingly as the service continued. Everything was normal until we began to sing some relatively new Scripture songs.

It was then I was astonished by something I had not noticed before. There seemed to be two congregations—one was singing, the other was not. The one was made up of middle–age couples, children, teenagers, college students, young married couples; numbering 150 or so. The other consisted of about 75 senior saints. Although this group had actively participated in the music to that point, when we got to the Scripture songs, it seemed there was a sign that read, "No one over 65 can sing a Scripture song."

My music ministry attention was definitely aroused. After the church service, I asked the pastor about it. He confirmed my observations and confessed that one of the reasons I was hired as a part–time Minister of Music and Worship was to meet the worship needs of the senior saints. The pastor shared that from the beginning of his attempts to renew the church's program of music and worship, the senior saints, for the most part, had refused to participate. He was unsure of what to do.

The majority of the congregation was supportive of the pastoral staff's attempt to renew the church's music and worship practices. But the older members felt ignored. They wanted a more traditional emphasis in worship services, singing the hymns and gospel songs they learned as children. They did not want any of "this new contemporary stuff." It did not seem to matter they were in the minority.

It was quite a dilemma for a new minister of music and the senior pastor. Prior to my coming, the pastor had preached on worship, introduced new songs of worship, taught Bible lessons on worship, and spent hours in personal worship. But this relatively small group of older men and women were not about to change their minds. They liked the Sunday morning worship service just like it had been for years: two songs, a choir special, the offertory, a solo, the sermon, and a song of invitation.

Principles of a Renewed Emphasis on Music and Worship

To solve the problems faced in my new congregation, I had to answer a basic question: "What are the principles of establishing a renewed emphasis on music and worship in a local church?" I discovered four key principles for renewing the music and worship program of a local church.

First, *you must be committed to discovering (or rediscovering) personal worship*. You must believe in the priority of worship and praise yourself before anyone will follow you in the experience. Ask God to teach you what true worship is all about. It is hypocritical to preach or teach about worship and to lead in public worship if we do not make worship an important component within our daily lives. You will not learn how to worship by just reading books on the subject but by practicing it.

Second, *worship must be taught*. Most people need to be taught what the Bible says about worship. People should be encouraged to read for themselves what God has said about worship. Worship needs to be taught in your sermons, your Sunday school lessons, your Bible studies, and in your home. This concept is especially crucial when seeking to lead a congregation whose understanding of worship may be more cultural and traditional than biblical.

Three, *communicate clearly to the congregation what you are trying to do and why you are doing it*. Change is threatening to everyone, but more so for those who have worshiped in the same basic pattern for years. Keep in mind, good communication will not necessarily prevent all criticism. No matter how well you communicate worship changes in advance, there will be someone who will not like them. However, good communication can go a long way to defuse potentially negative situations from developing.

Fourth, *music and worship should involve the entire body of Christ*. Music and worship should be a shared experience, not a performance. Worship is not just something for those who are musically gifted or those who are more comfortable in a visible leadership role. Worship is not just for adults, while teenagers and children watch. No! Worship is designed to be experienced by everyone!

Elements in a Worship Service

Part of the process of worship education is teaching your people the role each element of your services plays in creating an atmosphere for true worship to take place. Thus, worship is not seen as something done within the church service, but the entire service, and every element within it, is viewed properly as worship to the Lord. As people understand the function of each worship element, they will begin to actively worship through each part of the services.

Music makes up a large portion of many worship services. The remaining chapters in this book emphasize the role of music in the worship process. While music is an important part of worship, there are other elements which are a vital part as well.

Welcome and Announcements

Too often we include elements in our worship time that really cannot be called adoration, praise or exaltation of God. These activities are important to the body life of the church, but they are not worship. Such is the case with the Welcome and Announcements. For many, announcements tend to block the flow of worship as they direct our focus to the person making the announcements instead of directing our focus on God. For these reasons, I have found it helpful to put the announcements at the beginning or end of the service. Likewise, a time of Welcome to visitors is important, but not during the middle of a series of songs, Scripture and prayers of worship. The "welcome time" may become a very special opportunity for honoring visitors. At our church, our pastor honors the visitors by asking members and those already faithful in attending to stand "in honor of our guests." The ushers distribute visitor or registration cards to those seated. The visitors are asked to complete the card and place it in the offering plate later in the service. At the conclusion of this proclamation, the pastor usually asks everyone to stand, turn to a neighbor, and welcome them to the church. It is a fun time, a great opportunity for making new friends, and a non–threatening way to include visitors in the service.

Prayer

Quality time should be spent in each service praying to God. At leat three types of prayer should be utilized: prayers of confession, praise, and intercession. The first type of prayer in a worship service should be a prayer of confession. In Isaiah 6, Isaiah's first response to seeing the glory of God is to cry out, "Woe is me, for I am ruined! Because I am a man of unclean lips, and I live among a people of unclean lips; for my eyes have seen the King, the Lord of hosts" (v. 5). The person who is praying may wish to allow time for the people in the congregation to silently confess their sins to God. By placing such a prayer at the beginning of the worship experience, we emphasize the need of having "clean hands and a pure heart" as we "ascend into the hill of the Lord" (Ps. 24:3, 4).

Second, there should be prayers of praise. This is time spent thanking God for His goodness and for His marvelous works. You may wish to use one or more of the names given to God in the Old Testament (see the *Instructor's Guide* for a complete list). This is time set aside for the purpose of bragging on God. Prayers of praise do not need to be long or complicated. They should be simple, direct, and meaningful expressions of praise to God for who He is and what He had done and is doing.

A third kind of prayer in public worship is intercession for needs in the world around us and, most specifically, for the needs among the members of the congregation (Eph. 6:18; Phil. 4:6; 1 Tim. 2:1–8). Develop a policy on the collection of prayer requests, if you do not already have one (see *Instructor's Guide* for ideas). These three types of prayers may be used at different times in the service or may be combined into one prayer. Often, churches will utilize a "pastoral prayer" which will focus specifically on the needs of the congregation. Still others will incorporate the praying together of the Lord's Prayer at some point in the service.

The Word of God

Every service should have a time to focus attention on the Word of God. Passages can be read by one person as everyone else follows in their Bibles. The passage can be read in unison or responsively. A reader's theater style can be used if a passage has two or more characters. Or, two pastors can read responsively to each other.

The Creeds of the Church

Some churches will use one or more of the ancient creeds of the church in their worship services. Robert E. Webber, in *Worship Old & New*, defines a creed as the compression of "historical events in to a summary statement." A creed may be from the Bible itself, such as Deuteronomy 26:5–9, 1 Corinthians 15:3, 4, or 1 Timothy 3:16. Or, you may wish to use a creed from the early church, such as the Apostles' Creed (see *Instructor's Guide* for complete text). Creeds give an opportunity for the public affirmation of key doctrinal beliefs. A creed may be read in unison, responsively, or by a worship leader.

The Offering

The offering is viewed by some Christians as important but not necessarily a worshipful part of public services. Often, this opinion represents a lack of teaching on how God views our financial gifts as a way of offering sacrifices to Him (Phil. 4:18). The offering is a time to respond to God, giving back to Him part of what He has given to us. Even if a person does not have a financial gift to place in the offering plate, the congregation should be challenged to meditate on the giving of their lives completely and totally to God for His use (Rom. 12:1, 2).

The Ordinances of the Church

The ordinances of the church (some congregations refer to them as sacraments) are a vital part of worship. Evangelical churches practice baptism and the Lord's Supper (also called the Breaking of Bread, Communion, or the Eucharist) as ordinances. Some churches also include the washing of the saints' feet and/or the Agapé Feast as ordinances. Baptism, regardless of the mode your church practices, is an important event in the life of the person being baptized and should be a time for reflection and rejoicing on the part of the congregation.

The Lord's Supper is also an important worship element because the Church has been commanded to celebrate it (1 Cor. 11:23–26) and it symbolically represents the Gospel message. Some congregations will celebrate the Lord's Supper in every service, others will celebrate it on a monthly or quarterly basis. Regardless of the frequency, the Lord's Supper is a time of intimate worship as we meditate on the death and shed blood of Jesus for the remission of sins. Often, the celebration of the Lord's Supper will be a worship service within itself—with prayers, reading of Scripture, congregation hymns, responsive readings, and of course, the partaking of the Bread and Cup.

Creative Communication

Many evangelical churches effectively incorporate creative elements based on the service theme. Whatever the element, it should be evaluated on the same basis as other aspects of the service: Is the message biblical? Does the presentation draw attention to God or the mode of presentation? Does the creative form of communication lead the people into deeper worship?

The Sermon

Most evangelical worship services will have a time set aside for the preaching of the Word of God. This element is usually under the direct control of the pastoral staff. Although the sermon is focused on listening to God rather than speaking to God, it has always been a vital part of the evangelical worship experience.

The Closing

Many churches will use a hymn at the end of the sermon. This may be an *invitation*, a time to openly respond to Christ or to present themselves for church membership. For other churches, it may be called a *closing hymn*—a time to respond in song to the message that has just been preached. Still other churches will have a time of *meditation*, usually involving a choral or instrumental number.

The Benediction

Most services are closed by a "benediction," the Latin word for blessing. Typically the pastor or worship leader (perhaps raising one or both hands) will quote a short Bible passage or a prayer.

Special Elements

From time to time you may wish to incorporate worship elements that are special and out of the ordinary. It may be an infant dedication/baptism, the commissioning service of a missionary, or someone's ordination to the ministry. These special occasions can be worship as well, not something "squeezed into" an already–full order of service.

To Sum It Up

As a church begins renewal of its music and worship, people will discover that worship is a vital part of who we are. Teaching on worship answers key questions about congregational involvement.

For Further Discussion

1. How many different "congregations" in your church can you identify as to worship preferences? List some ways these different "congregations" can be brought together through renovation of the worship program.
2. What are some additional elements of your church's worship services not mentioned in this chapter?

For Application

1. Write down the "normal" order of service in an average worship service at your church. If you had the authority to change it, what changes would you make and why?
2. Design the rough outline of a four–week course on worship to be offered during the adult Sunday school hour. What elements would you include in such a course?

Principles for Renewing Music & Worship — Part 2

9

Singing does at least as much as preaching to impress the Word of God upon people's minds. Ever since God first called me, the importance of praise expressed in song has grown upon me.
—D. L. Moody

There really were two congregations attending the same service in the same building. They were identified primarily by age, with about 65 being the dividing line. In short, the older congregation did not like the changes in the worship services. To them, all the changes were being made to cater to the "younger crowd."

It was obvious the feelings went deep and there were not any simple solutions. I found myself asking, "How do I introduce new songs in a way that shows respect for more traditional songs which are both artistically and theologically profound? How do I develop worship forms broad enough to minister to a congregation that spans several generations?"

The older group's lack of interest in new worship forms was troubling. As I began to assess the situation, I discovered that while the younger group enjoyed the new worship songs, they were totally insensitive to the needs of the older members. Meanwhile, the older believers, who consistently "paid the bills" and were faithful in attendance, seemed to have little appetite for innovative forms of worship. Although the church was reaching new people, the senior saints still did not like what was happening to "their" worship services, musically or otherwise.

To discover a solution to the situation, I began to spend time with the senior saints in informal settings. As I began to really listen, I discovered they had some legitimate concerns with the changes in worship services. For starters, many were simply uncomfortable with the new songs. But it was not dislike of the new songs as much as it was an unfamiliarity with them. They felt left out. To them, it seemed the rest of the church did not regard "their music" as important enough to be included in the regular services. And there were some physical problems, too. The print on the transparencies used in singing choruses was too small to read. The new hymnals were too heavy for their aging muscles. They did not like to stand for long periods of time. My challenge was clear. What was the best way to meet everyone's spiritual, musical, and physical needs—in one worship service?

I remember the Sunday when the situation began to change. I used the old Black Gospel song, *Precious Lord, Take My Hand*, as a congregational song following a significant time of worship. Suddenly, I noticed the entire congregation was singing, old and young alike. So, the next week, I used another Black Gospel song, *Just A Closer Walk with Thee*, in a similar fashion. In the weeks to follow I began to use an older hymn in place of one of the newer Scripture songs. I realized these older gospel songs could be rearranged, modified, and used as worship and praise songs. The senior saints loved it. The younger ones thought I had found a body of new songs for expressing praise. A potentially volatile situation had been diffused. Through the power of meaningful music and worship, two separate congregations were being knit into one.

Planning for Worship

I discovered the hard way that it takes an investment of time to plan meaningful worship services, to meet the needs of a diverse congregation, to select suitable worship activities, and to seek a balance of both tradition and innovation. But it is time well spent! Our responsibility as worship leaders is to bring people from the busy clamor of the world to the throne of God. We will not be facilitators of God's grace if we rush through the process and hastily "throw something together" and call it worship.

Thus, be sure to block out plenty of time for planning. It takes time to prepare innovative worship experiences, to make transparencies or Powerpoint™ slides, to prepare song sheets, to rehearse with those responsible for the music, to practice other worship elements, and to communicate regularly with the senior pastor and/or worship team. There is no way around it—a good worship ministry demands time and a lot of it.

Personal Worship in Planning for Corporate Worship

Invest time in personal worship and praise when planning a worship service. Worship the Lord during the planning process. Literally go through the service with the Lord. Pray to Him at the times you have designated for congregational prayer. Read aloud the selected Scripture. Sing each song to the Lord as you plan. Planning for worship can become worship!

Consider the Purpose for the Service

Ask the following questions as you begin to plan:

What are the goals of the service?

What do you believe God wants to accomplish through this service? The pastoral leadership of the church must answer this question. You should also ask three additional questions: What does God want His people *to think* about and learn as a result of the service? What does God want His people *to feel* during the service? What does God want His people *to do* as a result of the service? Worship should minister to people intellectually, emotionally, and volitionally. If any one of these three focuses are absent, the congregation will be shortchanged.

Obviously, this approach demands that the pastor plan his sermons and worship goals several weeks, perhaps even months, in advance. The pastor should provide the worship leader or worship team with the texts, subjects, and basic approaches he will use as far in advance as possible. Also, he should share dates of special services or additional worship elements. While some would argue long–range planning hinders spontaneity and discourages the "leading of the Spirit" during a worship service, often just the opposite is true. Furthermore, if we truly believe that God is all–powerful and all–knowing, He can lead us just as effectively weeks or months ahead of time as He can during the service itself.

How much time is allocated for the total service, minus the sermon?

The time element will vary from congregation to congregation and may vary from service to service within the same congregation. The worship leaders need to know the time parameters. Is the service to be 45 minutes long? One hour long? Ninety minutes long? Two hours or more?

What worship elements should be used in the service, in what order, and what time frame?

First, the planners must choose the elements which will be part of the service. These elements will include: instrumental preludes and postludes, singing, reading of Scripture, giving of offerings, testimonies, prayer, thanksgiving, creative forms of communication such as drama, and the ordinances of the church (baptism and the Lord's Table). Then, decide how much time should be blocked out for each one. As you plan, keep in mind there is no one "way" to "do worship." God is a God of variety within unity. There are a wide range of worship forms and styles with which God is pleased. God does not want us to focus on the forms of worship as much as He desires us to focus on Him and Him alone.

Designing a Worship Service

The person who is responsible for planning the worship services of a church will vary from congregation to congregation. In a small congregation, the planning may be done by the pastor alone or the pastor working with the music minister/worship leader. Other churches may have a worship committee or team that will work with one or more members of the pastoral staff to plan the services. While it is possible for one person to plan the services, it is usually better to use a team approach.

There are a number of important steps in establishing a worship service planning routine:

1) There should be a regular time and place to meet. This may be at the church building or in someone's home. Either way, there should be easy access to worship resources (listed in #5 below).

2) Time should be spent at the beginning of the session in prayer for God's guidance in the process.

3) Some time should be spent evaluating the most recent worship services (use a form like the one in the *Instructor's Guide*). What worked? What did not work? What should be kept? What should be omitted? What needs to be modified? Since designing worship services is more of an art than a science, a time of evaluation will be quite helpful. Seek to learn from your failures as well as your successes.

4) The pastor should provide information as to the subjects, themes, and texts of upcoming sermons, as well as any special activities (such as baptism, infant dedication/baptism, missionary commissioning service, etc.).

5) Music and worship resources should be available: hymnals, song books, choir music (at least one piece of each song or collection), and any prayer books or other liturgical guides your church may use.

6) A keyboard is helpful for playing segments of various music pieces to better understand where it could fit in the order of service. A tape or CD player is also helpful for listening to any sound tracks you plan to use.

7) A planning guide (such as the sample in the *Instructor's Guide* or you may wish to design your own) can be used throughout the process.

8) After completing your planning guide, provide copies for everyone who needs them. Do not forget to give the proper information to the person responsible for your church's printed order of service (if you have one).

9) Carefully plan needed choir rehearsals.

Pacing of the Service

As you plan the music of a worship service, keep in mind there should be a balance between fast, medium, and slow songs. Once you have moved from a fast song to a slower one, it is wise not to go back to a fast song. It is usually better to save the slowest songs for later in the service. Care should be given not to drag out a worship service. It is essential not to rush through it either.

Transitions should be smooth. Changing keys between songs should be played by the pianist, organist, or keyboardist. If your musicians do not play by ear or do not know how to make key changes, write them out or purchase a "key change grid." Several companies publish chorus and hymn books with key changes already written between hymns. An appropriate word, song, or prayer can tie different sections of the service together.

Obtain the Right Tools

Every good carpenter must have the right tools. Inadequate or missing tools only prohibit progress in the building process. So it is with the music ministry. The use of the right tools will facilitate the worship experience. First, make sure everyone has access to words and music of the songs, and as well as the words of Scripture or any other material which will be read by the congregation. Some churches use Powerpoint™ slides, transparencies, and/or song sheets in place of the hymnal. However, before you decide to do away with a hymnal, be aware recently–produced hymnals include many of the popular, newer songs.

If you use slides or transparencies, be sure to have good projection equipment. The words on the screen must be clearly visible from the back–row seats. Obtain permission to reprint the text to songs. *Christian Copyright Licensing International* (CCLI) provides a service whereby churches can obtain permission to reprint words for use with transparencies and song sheets at a relatively low cost, based on the size of the congregation (see *Instructor's Guide* for more information).

Second, determine if the sound equipment is adequate for your facility and in good repair. Few things can hinder the flow of a worship service as an inadequate sound system. If you use sound tracks that require tape/CD players, have the equipment serviced on a regular basis.

Third, consider using an electronic keyboard in the services in addition to the traditional piano and organ. In fact, the more instruments you can utilize, the more people will be involved in participatory worship.

Fellowship Within the Worship Service

I have found it very fulfilling to structure a time of fellowship within a worship service. Sometimes it simply involves turning to a person next to you and shaking hands. At other times it may involve people seeking out a friend or family member to express appreciation, love, and concern. Ask the instrumentalist to play something up–tempo during these welcome times. It is best not to ask people to sing during a fellowship time. At other times, you may wish not to use music at all so the instrumentalists can participate in the activity. The whole idea is to provide a time for people to share with one another as they begin to share with God.

Closing

If your church has a public invitation (stepping forward for prayer or confession) or a few moments devoted to reflection or meditation after the sermon, it is appropriate to use hymns and songs of praise to augment the experience. Many churches only use gospel hymns in the *Just As I Am* tradition for the invitation time. Many other gospel hymns, however, are suitable for invitation and reflection.

Questions About Renewing Music and Worship

Here are some key questions commonly asked by those responsible for leading worship:

How can I lead renewal in music and worship with people who have not used newer forms of worship and are not sure they want to try?

Changing the traditional pattern of worship is a difficult task. It takes time to educate people and to become aware of their concerns. Your focus should be on providing a balance in the worship experience. Start with songs, Scripture, prayer, and giving in a manner already familiar to the situation. Begin teaching worship concepts to your choir and small groups or soloists. Introduce new songs through the children's choir ministries, youth choir, adult choir, soloists, or small groups.

One of the best resources in rejuvenating your church's worship services is your pastor. Encourage the pastor to prepare a series of sermons on the subject of worship and praise (more helps are listed in the *Instructor's Guide*).

I am in a very conservative church. Our church has had the same worship pattern for many years. How do I have an innovative music and worship service without using new music?

Do not forget the way people worship is often as much for cultural and historical reasons as scriptural ones. Thus, it is usually not possible to suddenly change the traditional way of worship and have the majority of people like it. Start by finding older songs that will work as worship and praise alternatives to newer songs. Find or write new tunes to be sung with the old texts. Do not draw attention to the introduction of new forms of music and worship ("Okay. We have had enough of these old songs. Now it is time to really worship the Lord."). In some older congregations, you may wish to begin by introducing changes on Sunday night first, before changing the Sunday morning service.

How do I introduce new forms of music and worship and still keep the focus evangelistic?

Among evangelical churches, there is a wide variety of approaches to evangelism within worship services. For some churches, no service is complete without a public invitation to respond to Christ's call for the new birth. Other churches encourage people to respond after the service by speaking to a pastor or elder. Still other churches view evangelism as something which should be encouraged only in services designated for that purpose. Regardless of the approach taken by your church, a renewed emphasis on music and worship should never detract from evangelism but in fact, will add to it. Although worship is primarily for believers, God can use a worship service to speak to the heart of the person who is not His child.

How do I involve the entire congregation in music and worship?

Variety is a key concept. Use different kinds of songs. Use the adult choir as a worship team. If your church has a graded choir program, you can use different choirs on a regular basis in worship services. Use instrumental solos and groups. Make a special effort to involve the non–musicians throughout each service. Non–musicians can lead in prayer, read the words to a hymn, share an inspirational hymn story, lead a responsive reading, present announcements, read the Scripture, or share a personal testimony. Involve entire families whenever possible.

How do I have a creative music and worship service when my church does not have a worship band?

The small congregation without an accomplished pianist, should consider one of the new products, available through Christian bookstores, which connect to electronic keyboards with MIDI capability. These components have the capability of playing hundreds of hymns as well as contemporary praise and worship songs. The operator can change the tempo, key, voice (instrument), number of verses, length of introduction, and can key in an entire order of service (see the *Instructor's Guide* for more information).

In a small church with only one or two musicians, you may wish to substitute an electronic keyboard for the piano. Most electronic keyboards have the potential for many voices (instruments) and can greatly add to the variety of the accompaniment.

If you have several pianists, the band parts can be played by a team of keyboard players. Use your piano, organ, and synthesizer together: the piano serves as rhythm; the organ can serve as a filler between songs; the electronic keyboard can play the instrumental (strings, brass, woodwinds) parts.

To Sum It Up

Worship leaders should prayerfully seek God's direction in planning for worship. In planning worship services, one should consider the goals of the service, the time alloted for the total service, and the time alloted for each element within the service? As you design a worship service, note the pacing, transitions, available tools, and special elements. Each element of the worship service should fit together to maximize the worship and praise of God.

For Further Discussion

1. If you were assigned the responsibility of planning the worship services of your church, what procedure would you use, who would you recruit to help you, and why?
2. What elements should be a part of every worship service? Why? What elements should be considered optional parts of every worship service? Why?
3. In the ideal situation, what worship resources should be available to those who are planning the services?

For Application

1. Using the sample evaluation form in the *Instructor's Guide* for this course, evaluate the worship services you will attend between now and the next class meeting. Be prepared to compare notes with your classmates.
2. If possible, examine back copies of your church's bulletin (if it contains the order of service). Can you detect a thematic approach to worship? If so, what are the themes that emerge from the various elements of the service (not including the sermon)?
3. In a small group of two to five people, plan four worship services using the guidelines in this chapter.

Building an Effective Program of Music & Worship – Part 1

10

I wept at the beauty of your hymns and canticles, and was powerfully moved at the sweet sound of your Church singing. These sounds flowed into my ears, and the truth streamed into my heart.
—Augustine

Over the years I have worked with some of the most talented and accomplished church music programs—and probably some of the worst. I have worked in churches with large, well–funded programs and I have worked with music programs that were small and struggling. Some churches had music ministries where everyone was committed to excellence (the size of the church was not a factor) and others seemed to be satisfied with mediocrity. On each occasion, I have considered it an honor to serve with the music and worship ministry. For the most part, every music program—from the largest, most progressive to the smallest with the fewest resources—has faced the same three challenges:

✔ they did not have a clear idea of the status of the music and worship ministry in the eyes of the congregation;

✔ they did not have a clear vision of where they believed God wanted the music and worship ministry to go;

✔ they did not have an action plan in place to lead them to fulfill that vision.

A Five–fold Task

I have sought to build music and worship ministries in local churches on a five–fold foundation. In brief, the music/worship leader has a task to teach, train, edify, evangelize, and support all the ministries of the local church through the ministry of music and worship.

74

Teach

The music/worship leader should teach concepts of ministering through music, music literature, and music fundamentals. But the music/worship leader's main focus should be on teaching the Word of God through the ministry of music and worship. Thus, music/worship leaders must not only be musicians, they must also be Bible teachers.

Train

Training is leading people to apply what they have been taught. The music/worship leader should train people in the how to's of the music and worship program. Choir rehearsals and other practices should be training experiences. The music/worship leader has the responsibility of training people to fulfill their potential as singers, worship leaders, song directors, conductors, teachers—to be ministers themselves!

Edify

Edification is essentially the process of building up people. Encouragement is a large part of that process. Through the ministry of music, people should be encouraged to grow in their faith, to explore ways of involvement in the various ministries of the local church and ultimately, to become more like Christ.

Evangelize

The fourth task for the music/worship leader is to proclaim the Gospel through the ministry of music and worship. As we evangelize through music, we are fulfilling Psalm 96. Evangelism through music and worship may happen as a choir, group, or individual from your church presents a program of music at a local mall, participates in a radio or television ministry, holds services at a retirement home, provides music for a prison ministry and other outreach activities. Wherever there are people who do not know Christ, music can be used as a tool of evangelization.

Support

The music/worship leader should seek to support all the various ministries of the church through the music and worship ministries. By its very nature, music and worship touches every member of the body of Christ. Every part of the church's life should be filled with music and worship. Supporting the church body can happen in a variety of ways. It may mean providing special music for a wedding or a funeral. It could be providing music for a community–wide Easter sunrise service or a church conference.

With these five tasks in mind, ask these questions:
- ✓ What is the current status of your church's music and worship program?
- ✓ What vision does your church have for the music and worship program of the future?
- ✓ What is your plan of action to get there?

Evaluate

Suppose you are planning to drive to a store in your area that you have never visited. To make sure you know how to get there, you call ahead to ask for directions. The first question the person at the store will ask is, "From where are you coming?" In other words, you cannot be given accurate directions on how to find the store if your starting location is not known. This principle is true in the ministry of the local church as well. You will have a difficult time developing an action plan for the music and worship ministry if you are unaware of exactly where the ministry is currently in your church. Thus, the careful evaluation of your present program is the first step in renewing a program of music and worship.
- ✓ Where has your music and worship ministry been in the past?
- ✓ How effective is the music and worship ministry in your church?
- ✓ What are the strengths and weaknesses of your music and worship ministry?
- ✓ What are the music and worship needs and wants of your people?
- ✓ What resources are available in personnel, facility, and finances for the ministry of music and worship?
- ✓ What can be learned from the evaluation process that will help your music and worship program triumphantly face the future?

The *Instructor's Guide* for this course includes a full–length *Music and Worship Evaluation Form* to guide you through the process. Although this evaluation form can be completed by a pastor, music/worship leader, or a worship team, it is often helpful to have the assistance of a trained, experienced music/worship leader to interpret the results of your evaluation. This resource person can also assist your church in implementing an action plan to renew your ministry of music and worship.

The *Music and Worship Evaluation Form*—will focus your attention on these areas:

1. Leadership of the Music and Worship programs—Examine the leadership structure of your music and worship program. Evaluate the effectiveness of a music/worship council (board, committee, team). Specifically state changes to increase its effectiveness. Develop written ministry descriptions for each leadership position if none exist.

2. *Programs (Adult choir, children's choir, orchestra, worship band, etc.)*
List programs currently in place. Rate each of those programs from 1
(poor) to 10 (excellent). Rate the strengths and weaknesses of each
program. Determine needed improvements for each program. List
new programs to be added.

Part of this step of the evaluation is to conduct a church–wide
survey to determine how people view the music and worship ministry and their perceived needs (a sample survey is included in the
Instructor's Guide). This music survey will also gather information
regarding the music and worship gifts, skills, and experiences of the
members of your congregation as well as tracking involvement patterns of participants.

3. *Budget*—Assess the current budget for music and worship in dol-
lars. In percentage to the total church giving and ministry goals,
determine if the music and worship ministry is underfunded.

4. *Space and Equipment*—Diagram your worship facility, storage
space, and rehearsal areas. Note proposed improvements as well as
current equipment coverage.

5. *Goals and Objectives*—State the goals and objectives of the overall
ministry of music and worship clearly and concisely. The goals and
objectives of smaller music groups will need to complement the
church as a whole.

Envision

Once you have carefully evaluated, you will have a good idea of
where you have been and a picture of where the leadership and people
of the church want to go. The envisioning process is for the church
leadership to agree upon the music and worship needs (both real
and perceived) of the congregation.

Specific ministry goals and objectives for the overall music and
worship ministry should be developed based on what has been learned
from the evaluation.

Each agency within the ministry of music and worship should
be encouraged to develop small ensembles, solo/group ministries,
regular concert series, or evenings of praise.

The results of the congregation–wide music survey should be
utilized to identify the people who are gifted in various music and
worship areas and to plug them into current ministries.

As the leadership plans for the future, carefully look at the individual ministries that make up the music and worship program of your
church.

The Congregational Ministry

When developing a vision for the congregational ministries of music and worship, consider the leadership, the instrumentalists, and the resources for congregational singing. Knowing how many people are available to lead congregational singing and worship, who they are, the scope of their abilities, their available time, and their willingness to be a part of the ministry is essential information (see the *Instructor's Guide* for how to train congregational song leaders). The availability of instrumentalists, the level of skill, and willingness to participate are critical scheduling issues. Resources include instruments, sound systems, hymnals, chorus sheets, transparencies/Powerpoint™ slides (and projectors), and any other items needed to support the music and worship ministry.

The Choral Ministry

Every area of the choral ministry—children, adult, senior citizen, and small ensemble—has a set of ministry needs including: knowing the leadership base, being aware of the quantity and potential of singers, having enough accompanists, and tapping into needed resources (equipment, printed music, and an adequate budget). Good keyboard instruments are a must for practice areas.

Building an Instrumental Program

Instrumental ministries take time to develop and usually involve much more detail work than choral ministry. Some music/worship leaders are afraid to launch into an instrumental program because they are not familiar with a variety of instruments. Sometimes they are inexperienced in conducting larger groups. Some music/worship leaders resist having an instrumental ensemble because there may not be enough players to cover all the printed parts. However, in many cases, especially when using strings, electronic keyboards can fill in quite well for traditional instruments. The important thing is to provide opportunities for those who have instrumental talents.

Begin with a small group performing once a month. Keep the music relatively simple. As the group gains more experience, move on to more difficult music and provide more opportunities to play. Use instrumentalists as soloists for offertories and preludes. Be on the lookout among the church's children for potential musicians. As younger musicians develop their skills, they can serve as music library assistants, section leaders, keepers of instruments, and even rehearsal time babysitters.

Hand–bell choirs can be excellent additions to the music ministry of your church. While requiring a substantial investment up front, hand-bells when carefully maintained can last for many years. A hand–bell choir can provide additional opportunities for ministry involvement.

Music Resources

An inventory of equipment, supplies, and printed music relating to the music and worship program should be made, if not already available. The greatest resource of your music and worship program is people. For a music and worship ministry to be successful, it cannot be centered in a handful of musicians. Everyone in the church must feel welcomed to participate. Provision should be made for people to serve even if they do not have musical abilities. Music/worship leaders will often need to provide child care for special rehearsal times (and be willing to budget the funds for this service). The key to successful ministry is involvement. Provide opportunities for your people to utilize their gifts and skills in the ministry of music and worship.

To Sum It Up

The music/worship leader has a five-fold task—to fully utilize the ministry of music and worship to teach, train, edify, evangelize, and support the ministries of the local church. When establishing or renewing a ministry of music and worship, the first step is to evaluate the current situation. After a careful evaluation, the church leadership must envision where God is leading their ministry of music and worship. Every aspect of the music and worship program should be included in the envisioning process: the congregation, the choral ministry, the instrumental program, and the resources that are available to the congregation.

For Further Discussion

1. Do you believe there are any more responsibilities of the music/worship leader in addition to the five mentioned in this chapter? If so, what are they?
2. What are some worthy goals for a music and worship program?
3. Why is it important to gain God's vision for your church's music and worship program?

For Application

1. Set up a sample timetable for completing an evaluation of your church's music and worship ministries.
2. What are the current resources of your church's music and worship ministry? What additional resources are needed?
3. What are some potential ministries of music and worship that your church should consider adding to its program in the future?

Building an Effective Program of Music & Worship – Part 2

11

What is to reach the heart must come from above, if it does not come thence, it will be nothing but notes—body without spirit.
— Ludwig van Beethoven

Imagine that you have decided to buy a house. Like many people, a clause in the sales contract gives you the right to have the home inspected for any structural problems. So, you hire a qualified home inspector to do a thorough inspection of the home. You arrive the day of the inspection to walk through the house with the inspector. You watch as he checks the various parts of the house—the plumbing system, the electrical system, the heating and cooling systems, the insulation, and so on.

After the inspection, you receive a copy of the report, which details the condition of the house and recommends any repairs that should be made before you close on the purchase. At this point you have several options. You may decide the repairs are too extensive and cancel the sales contract or you may ask the owner to make the needed repairs and complete the sale. It is hard to believe that anyone would exercise a third option—go through with the sale but not make any of the recommended repairs.

How does this relate to the music and worship program of your church? Once you have evaluated the current status of your music and worship program and have gone through the process of envisioning what it could be with God's help, you are then faced with similar options. Since you most likely will not decide to close your church down, which of the remaining two options is the best choice? Will you discover the price of change too high to pay and continue in the status quo? Or will you adopt an action plan to implement the changes suggested by your evaluation and your envisioning? While evaluating and envisioning are important steps in renewing your church's music and worship ministry, without the third step in the process, the enacting of an action plan, all the work to this point will be in vain.

Planning Prerequisites

No organization can be successful for long without a plan. The following is a general approach to establishing or renewing a ministry of music and worship. There are three prerequisites you should keep in mind as you develop and enact an action plan.

Be Respectful

You should be respectful of the people you have been called to serve. In many cases, there are church members who have labored unselfishly without pay for years in the music and worship ministry of your church. Allow your people to help establish priorities for your church. Make sure those priorities are based on meaningful goals with your people serving as active participants in setting those goals. Include the three "seeks" in your planning: Seek their opinion. Seek to meet their expectations. Seek innovative ways to include everyone in the planning process.

Be Realistic

Make it a point to get to know your people and their talents well. Find creative ways to learn more about their interests. Devise ways to accommodate those interests. Be realistic about their talents. Make it a point to know their gifts as musicians, communicators, educators, leaders, and creative personnel. Try to be realistic when determining how fast changes in the music and worship program should be introduced.

Be Responsible

Be responsible for finding out what will genuinely meet your people's needs. Seek to meet your people where they are. If they cannot read music, find a way to communicate and perform with them so they do not feel threatened by your approach to music ministry. Be patient. A successful music and worship ministry will not be built quickly. It will take time. Everyone will not endorse immediately everything you are trying to accomplish. Be persistent. Do not give up or give in to discouragement. If you have clearly communicated your goals, objectives, plans and approaches to ministry, God will be honored in the long run.

Steps in the Planning Process

The process of planning ahead is sometimes easier when using a guide already designed as an aide to worship leaders. Many churches use *The Lectionary* with thematic material outlined according to the church year. Several music publishers and denominational music groups sell planning resources.

Step 1: Music and Worship Leader

Designate who has the overall responsibility for the music and worship programs of your church. The music/worship leader should maintain an active and meaningful relationship with the senior pastor, the total church body, and all of the people who are involved in the music and worship ministry.

Step 2: Music and Worship Council

Consider the organization of a music council (you may wish to call it a committee, board, or team) if your church does not currently have one in place. The purpose of a council is to provide administrative and philosophical support to the music/worship leader. You may wish to consider holding an annual planning retreat with the music council. A retreat allows members of the council to get away from their normal routines to concentrate on the music and worship activities of the coming year.

The music council should also deal with matters relating to various music and worship policies. Ideally, personnel for the music council should include representatives of the music and worship staff: the music/worship leader (usually the chairperson), all directors of other choirs (children's, youth, hand–bells, senior citizens, etc.), the major accompanists (pianists, organist), and the lead sound technician. It is also helpful to have one or two members–at–large elected as representatives from the performing groups.

Step 3: Music and Worship Calendar

Take time to review the calendar of events for the coming year. A music and worship calendar should be used to schedule rehearsals, performances, special services, solo and group performances, choir meetings, group gatherings, educational workshops, leadership meetings, and special events. It should be correlated with the church's master calendar. It will allow leaders to communicate with ministry participants and schedule practices and services in an efficient and timely manner. The calendar should be sent to all music and worship participants on a monthly or quarterly basis.

Step 4: Ministry Descriptions

Ministry descriptions should be developed for each position in the music and worship program. In some cases a church will require formal approval of these ministry descriptions by the congregation or a church board. Ministry descriptions should be realistic. Involve the people currently holding these positions in writing their own ministry descriptions. Positions needing a ministry description include: music/worship leader, music ministry secretaries, members of the music council, directors of ensembles and small groups, children's choir directors, youth choir directors, instrumental ensemble directors, sponsors for each group, sanctuary choir officers, pianists, organist, keyboard players, sound technicians, lighting personnel, and Powerpoint™ slide or transparency workers.

Step 5: Music Education

Establish and promote a program of music education. Training should be provided for the directors of various groups as well as for the program participants. The type and extent of training offered will depend on the skill levels of the individuals involved. The training curriculum may include music fundamentals, music theory, sight singing, concepts of worship, and the leading of congregational worship (more information on the leading of congregational singing is found in the *Instructor's Guide*). Specialized training for sound and light technicians should also be provided.

Step 6: Performing Components

Carefully examine each performing component of the music and worship ministry. One of the main components is the *sanctuary* or *adult choir*. Much of your music program revolves around the activities of this one large, totally–focused choral group. They should function as a large worship team. This group can, and should, serve as a core body of committed worship leaders that sing and minister throughout the year. When the congregation thinks of music, they should first think of a positive, affirming ministry of music from this group. Ensembles, small groups, and many soloists should come out of this choir. As the sanctuary choir grows, so will the total music and worship ministry of the church.

Accompanists include anyone serving as keyboard player, pianist, and organist. Accompanists are needed for congregational singing, choir rehearsals, special ensembles, small groups (trios, quartets, etc.), and solo presentations. Many churches do not have a large number of accompanists, but over time, a team of accompanists committed to ministry can be developed. It is imperative to invest time in developing young accompanists and to give them opportunities to play for singing groups. While you may not wish to use sound tracks as a primary source for choir, solo, and small group accompaniment, tracks and MIDI–assisted keyboard accompaniment offer alternatives to live accompaniment.

A growing church music program needs to have *age–graded choirs*. These may include children's music activities and choirs, youth choirs and traveling ensembles, youth instrumental groups, small ensembles, a sanctuary or "main" choir, and a senior adult music ministry. Each of these choirs will need a director, accompanist, and usually an assistant. This assistant may or may not be a member of the group but the idea is for them to help with attendance, library assignments, or serve as an instrumental music director.

Every church music and worship ministry (large or small) needs a *music secretary/librarian.* One or more persons to care for administrative details which may include ordering music, filing music, scheduling, and telephoning and communicating with all those involved in the music ministry. Often, many of these aspects of ministry go undone or are postponed to another time because the music/worship leader is overloaded with responsibilities.

To Sum It Up

Building an effective music and worship program starts with evaluation of where you are currently, envisioning what God desires for your future, and enacting an action plan. In the entire planning process, the music/worship leader should be respectful, realistic, and responsible to the congregation. After a church selects a music/worship leader, a music council should be established to assist in the ministry. A music and worship calendar is a must. Ministry descriptions can give needed guidance and cohesion to the entire music and worship ministry.

For Further Discussion

1. What are some of the potential problems a church can face in the planning process of renewing a music and worship ministry? How can these problems be avoided or overcome?
2. What are the positives and negatives of having a music council in your church?
3. What other positions, not mentioned in this chapter, are part of the music and worship ministry in your church?

For Application

1. Plan a hypothetical church music and worship calendar for the next 12 months.
2. If your church has ministry descriptions for those involved in the music and worship ministries of your church, distribute copies to the group. Do these descriptions identify specific tasks (times, activites, places, etc.)? How can these descriptions be improved?
3. Choose several positions in your church's music and worship ministry and write ministry descriptions for each one.

Do's in Renewing
a Music & Worship Ministry

1) Do spend plenty of time in prayer, asking God for wisdom in starting and maintaining a new emphasis on music and worship.
2) Do spend quality time reading what the Bible says about music and worship.
3) Do read and study books on the subject of music and worship. (See the bibliography.)
4) Do ask God to lead you into a closer walk and fellowship with Him.
5) Do have regular times of personal worship.
6) Do share your discoveries and experiences of worship with others.
7) Do seek to include all members of the body of Christ in music and worship.
8) Do preach and teach regularly about music and worship.
9) Do include representatives of the entire congregation in planning for music and worship.
10) Do remember that Satan is the enemy of music and worship. Satan loses when music and worship in the church are effective.

Don'ts in Renewing
a Music & Worship Ministry

1) Don't introduce new forms of music and worship to prove a point. God does not have to have new music and worship forms to reveal Himself to His people.
2) Don't force new forms of music and worship on your people. Wait on God's timing.
3) Don't exclude any group in the congregation. Worship is for everyone.
4) Don't limit yourself to just a few styles of music.
5) Don't allow fear of failure to interfere with a desire to renew the music and worship of your congregation (2 Tim. 1:7).
6) Don't be critical of those who are critical of you. It takes time to win the confidence of your people.
7) Don't be afraid to try new methods of expression of your love for God.
8) Don't expect people to like everything you do all the time.
9) Don't begin renewal of music and worship without investing time in planning.
10) Don't begin a new program of music and worship in your own strength.

Resources for
Music & Worship

12

*Music is God's gift to man, the only art of heaven given
to earth, the only art of earth we take to heaven.*
—Walter Savage Landor

Twelve chapters are not enough to cover every aspect of the ministry of music and worship. At the very least, however, this course has been designed to provide an historical overview of music and worship, a biblical foundation for both, and practical instruction on how to renew a local church's music and worship ministry. Regardless of the stage of development at your church, every program of music and worship needs resources. Sometimes, the most difficult part is knowing where to look and who to call. In this concluding chapter, a variety of music and worship resources are listed. While every effort has been made to insure the accuracy of the information, ETA is not connected with any of the companies listed nor does ETA give a blanket endorsement of all items produced and sold by each company. This information is provided solely to help you and your church locate the music and worship resources you need.

Selecting a Hymnal
For many churches, the hymnal is the most visible, and most used, music and worship resource. Hymnals provide a vast catalog of the Christian experience expressed through song—a printed record of church tradition. Hymnals are a resource tool for worship, a treasure chest of Christian doctrine, a book that encourages and edifies through psalms, hymns, and spiritual songs. As musical styles change and develop, so do the collection of hymns included in a particular hymnal. Today, there is a wide range of modern hymnals available with one to fit every style of worship. Some hymnals are published by specific denominations and church groups. Others are produced by independent publishers and are designed for broader church use.

With so many hymnals to choose from, how does a church make a wise purchasing decision? Here are ten things to look for when considering a hymnal.

1. Broad selection of tunes. A good hymnal should have a broad and diverse selection of songs including: traditional hymns, English hymnody, western European music, American folk, singing convention style, Scripture songs, youth choruses, and gospel hymn traditions. Selections should represent the scope of musical preferences within your congregation.

2. Theological and worship style compatibility. Carefully examine the hymnal to assess compatibility with your church. For example, a church with a free–form worship service would be frustrated with a hymnal designed for liturgical worship. Likewise, a liturgical church would not be well served by a hymnal omitting anthems.

3. Clear organization. The hymnal should be well organized and divided into chapter–like sections. Some hymnals are designed around a number of themes: adoration, confession, commitment, service, etc. Other hymnals are organized around doctrines such as God, Jesus Christ, the Holy Spirit, the Trinity, the Gospel, the Church, Christian living, salvation, and heaven. Special occasions such as Easter, Christmas, and other church year celebrations may also be identified.

4. Appropriate hymnological data. Each hymn should include the author and composer's names, names of translators and arrangers, the date of composition, designation of metrical rhythm (see #6 below), and tune name (see glossary). Some hymnals include a Scripture reference with the hymn.

5. Scripture readings. The hymnal should include a healthy group of Scripture readings on a variety of subjects. Be sure to check if the Bible versions used in the hymnal are compatible with your church's position.

6. Practical indexes. Most hymnals have a number of helpful indexes. Look for these indexes: hymn index (in alphabetical order); topical index (both for hymns and Scripture readings); metrical index of tunes (a numerical code allowing alternate tunes to be chosen for the hymn text); and an index of authors, composers, translators, and arrangers. Some hymnals include an index of Scripture readings arranged in book order and an index of Scripture allusions in the hymns. Hymnal indexes should be practical and easy to use.

7. Layout and design. Is the type easy to read for your older members? Are the words easy to follow, even for those who do not read music? Are the hymn numbers easy to locate for quick identification? Is the binding of high quality? Is the book easy to open and will it stay open for your accompanists? Is the hymnal available in several colors so as to complement your church's interior?

8. Size of the hymnal. Older members may find larger hymnals difficult to handle. Also make sure the hymnal will fit the pew rack.

9. Additional resources. Are additional resources available with the hymnal? Some hymnals have orchestrations, sound tracks, MIDI files, and even worship handbooks that provide background information to enhance appreciation of the hymns.

10. Buy within your budget. Hymnals vary in cost. Even though money will probably be a factor in your choice of hymnals, the least expensive hymnal may not be the best hymnal for your situation. Hymnals can be purchased through a Christian bookstore or a music distributor. Sometimes quantity discounts are available.

Rarely is the selection of a church hymnal a decision made by one or two people. Usually, it is a committee affair. It will take an investment of time to do an adequate evaluation and recommendation. If the hymnal you select is a good fit with your congregation, it should be able to meet the needs of your church for about ten years. A hymnal evaluation form is available in the *Instructor's Guide* which can assist in the selection process.

The following hymnals were designed for a broad evangelical audience.

The Celebration Hymnal
Word Music
3319 West End Ave., Ste. 201
Nashville, TN 37203
888–324–9673

Hymns for the Worshiping Church
Hope Publishing Company
380 S. Main Place
Carol Stream, IL 60188
800–323–1049

Hymns for the Family of God
Brentwood–Benson Music
741 Cool Springs Blvd.
Franklin, TN 37067
615–261–6300

The Rejoice Hymnal
Randall House Publishers
P.O. Box 17306
Nashville, TN 37217
615–361–1221

Print Music Resources

Over the last twenty–five years, publishers of Christian music have used an effective marketing tool called the "choral club." These clubs are specifically designed to assist local church music/worship leaders in evaluating music. For an annual fee, ranging from $15 to $100, music/worship leaders receive each new choral print and recording release from the publisher. Publishing companies usually send a sample of their music with a cassette, CD, or MIDI file. The music/worship leader listens to the audio recording of the music while reading through the print edition. This has proved a valuable resource for music/worship leaders as they are immediately made aware of new arrangements, styles, and concepts in music ministry.

Today, this is the primary source of communication between music publishers and music/worship leaders. Your church should seriously consider membership in one or more of these clubs. They can be the life–blood for continued growth and development of the music and worship ministries at your church. The following is a sample list of publishers and music distributors who offer some type of choral club. Additional resources are listed in the *Instructor's Guide.*

Choral Clubs

Brentwood–Benson Club
Brentwood–Benson Music
741 Cool Springs Blvd.
Franklin, TN 37067
800–846–7664

Integrity Music Church
 Resources
1000 Cody Road
Mobile, AL 36695
800–239–7000

Lillenas Choral Club
Lillenas Publishing
2923 Troost Ave.
Kansas City, MO 64109
800–239–7000

Other Sources of Printed Music

Baptist Spanish Publishing
 House
P.O. Box 4255
El Paso, TX 79914
915–566–9656

OCP Publications (Oregon
 Catholic Press)
P.O. Box 18030
Portland, OR 97218
800–528–6043

Kempke's Music Service
101 Gordon Street
Sanford, FL 32771
407–562–0333

Maranatha Music - California Office
2753 Camino Capistrano B1
San Clemente, CA 92672
949-940-7000

Copyrights

Music/worship leaders need to be aware that unauthorized photocopying of copyrighted music, even for the purpose of using it in a church service, is illegal. Unfortunately, many churches have broken the copyright law, justifying it on the basis of "saving the Lord's money." In an effort to remedy this situation, Christian Copyright Licensing, Inc. (CCLI) serves as a liaison between music publishers and local churches to provide churches a convenient way to fully comply with the copyright law. Basically, CCLI grants a license to a church that permits use of a song's text and music in bulletins, on slides/transparencies, for congregational songsheets, as well as covering tape duplication of worship services. CCLI charges an annual fee based on the size of the church.

WEB Site Resources

www.worshipflow.com

www.praisesongstore.com

www.nationalworshipleaderconference.com

christianmusic.suite101.com/article.cfm/christian sheet music websites

www.worshipdirector.org

www.1 christian.net

www.hymncharts.com

www.worshipmax.com

www.268generation.com/2.0/splash5.htm

www.worshiptogether.com

www.ccli.com/usa/default.aspx

www.worshipleader.com

www.ccmmagazine.com

MIDI Resources

One of the most exciting and innovative approaches to music ministry is the use of electronic keyboards that have MIDI interfaces. MIDI stands for *Music Instrument Digital Interface* and is a set of engineering standards which allow computers and musical instruments to communicate with each other. Many keyboards have built-in sequencers that allow for prerecorded compositions to be played through those instruments. Publishers produce disks with recorded data specifically designed to be read by sequencers. These disks, called MIDI files, may include full orchestrations, hymn tune arrangements, and a whole array of sound tracks designed to be played through MIDI instruments. Church musicians can use the technology of MIDI to create their own inexpensive sound tracks and accompaniment recordings.

> *www.gnms.com/software.htm*   *www.midimarvels.com*
> *www.ultimatemidi.com*

Choir Robes

Many churches utilize robes for choirs and/or pastors, especially for Sunday morning worship. Here are some of the companies who offer a variety of styles, fabrics, and prices for robes. You may also be able to order robes through your local Christian bookstore.

> Murphy Cap & Gown Co.
> 4200 31st Street N.
> St. Petersburg, FL 33714
> 800–876–8774
> *www.murphyrobes.com*
> Collegiate Apparel, *www.robes.com*

Additional Studies in Worship

If you are interested in doing further study in the areas of music and worship, use the bibliography, found at the end of this book, as a guide to books on the subject. Of special interest is the seven–volume set entitled *The Complete Library of Christian Worship*, published by Hendrickson Publishers.

The *Institute for Worship Studies* has been founded to serve as a training school for persons who lead worship and desire to learn more about the history, theology, and practice of worship. The courses from the *Institute* are all extension courses which can be studied at home and lead to the *Diploma of Worship Studies*. Write or call for more information.

The Institute for Worship Studies
P.O. Box 894
Wheaton, IL 60188
800–282–2977
www.instituteforworshipstudies.org

The Robbert Webber Institute
of Worship Studies
151 Kingsley Avenue
Orange Park, FL 32073
http://www.iwsfla.org/

Liberty University Center for Worship
1971 University Blvd.
Lynchburg, VA 24501
http://www.liberty.edu/academics/arts-sciences/worship/index.cfm?PID=11768

To Sum It Up

There are many resources for the music and worship ministries of the local church. The choice of a hymnal is an important decision for any church. Many publishers provide special programs for music/worship leaders to receive copies of new music on a regular basis. There are many publishers producing a variety of new music from a wide range of worship styles. The *Institute for Worship Studies* provides opportunities for further studies. CCLI provides an easy way to comply with copyright laws. In addition, there are Christian music periodicals, MIDI resources, and choir robes which can all enhance the ministry of music and worship.

For Further Discussion

1. What are some of the advantages and disadvantages of using a hymnal in church worship services?
2. What advice would you give to a church that has illegally copied printed music?
3. What are some areas of worship that you would like to study more about?

For Application

1. Ask someone in your church or a sister church, who uses a MIDI keyboard and computer, to demonstrate the capabilities of such a system.
2. Ask your music/worship leader to share samples of the various types of printed music currently available.
3. Analyze your church's hymnal utilizing the ten factors covered in this chapter.

Glossary

Baptistic structure – an emphasis on robust congregational singing with particular focus on the preaching of the Word followed by a public invitation.

charismatic structure – an exceptional openness to the Holy Spirit during worship activities.

copyright – a designation of ownership whereby the exclusive, legal right to reproduce, publish, and/or sell the material can be granted.

creed – an authoritative statement, or collection of statements, regarding doctrine held by an individual or religious body; often orally recited in the course of worship.

dirge – a song or hymn of grief used to accompany a funeral or memorial rites.

high church emphasis – liturgical worship structure involving creeds, sacraments, and the traditional practices of the Anglican Church.

hymnological data – all the identifying information about a hymn at the heading of a specific piece and/or the organizational information found in various indexes.

key change grid – designed as a chart, graph, or wheel, this musical aid provides an "at-a-glance" reference to chord progressions; used to modulate (change keys) within or between songs.

incantation – a written, recited, or sung formula designed for a specific effect.

lamentation – any act expressing sorrow or deep regret.

liturgical structure – prescribed form or manner of governing the words or actions for public worship.

low church emphasis – characterized by their concern for the spiritual and social welfare of individuals rather than the maintenance of tradition.

matrix – a form or structure from which something else originates or is developed.

metrical rhythm – related to tune names and usually identified with numbers at the heading of a hymn. The number of digits shown indicates the number of lines per stanza. Each digit indicates the number of syllables receiving an accent in each line of poetry.

MIDI – Musical Instrument Digital Interface.

modern-day lute – a stringed instrument with a pear-shaped body and a neck with a fretted fingerboard and a head with pegs for tuning.

percussion instruments – any musical instrument sounded by striking, shaking, or scraping.

rounded-note notation – based on a 7–note scale with rounded appearance given to musical notes; as opposed to "shaped-note" notation.

shaped-note notation – developed during the Revolutionary War period, a system of reading musical tones of a tetrachord by the shape of a musical note: a triangle for "fa," a circle for "sol," a square for "la," and a diamond for "mi." This is known as the "Fasola Tradition."

stringed instruments – any musical instrument sounded by plucking, striking, or drawing a bow across tense strings.

tempo – the rate of speed of a musical piece; up-tempo meaning "faster."

tune name – in the early days of publishing, only words appeared in hymnals. A song leader would announce a hymn text to be sung to a particular tune, often named after the composer, location of the hymn writing, a person to whom it was dedicated, or other functional designation.

wind instruments – any musical instrument sounded by wind; especially the breath of the player.

Bibliography

Allen, Ronald Barclay, and Gordon Borror. *Worship—Rediscovering the Missing Jewel of the Church*. Portland, OR: Multnomah Press, 1982.*

Boschman, LaMar. *A Passion for His Presence*. Shippensburg, PA: Revival Press, 1932.*

Davies, J. G. *The Westminster Dictionary of Worship*. Philadelphia, PA: Westminster Press, 1972.*

Delamont, Vic. *The Ministry of Music in the Church*. Chicago, IL: Moody Press, 1980.*

Eskew, Harry, and Hugh T. McElrath. *Sing with Understanding*. Nashville, TN: Broadman Press, 1980.

Gordon, W.C. ed. "History of Gospel Music" *American Gospel Magazine*, May–June, 1992.

Hayford, Jack. *Worship His Majesty*. Waco, TX: Word, Inc., 1987.

Hustad, Donald P. *Jubilate! Church Music in the Evangelical Tradition*. Carol Stream, IL: Hope Publishing Company, 1981.

Lovelace, Austin C., and William C. Rice. *Music and Worship in the Church*. Nashville, TN: Abingdon, 1976.

Lunde, Alfred E. *Christian Education Thru Music*. Wheaton, IL: Evangelical Training Association, 1978.*

MacArthur, John F., Jr. *The Ultimate Priority*. Chicago, IL: Moody Press, 1983.

Mapson, J. Wendell. *The Ministry of Music in the Black Church*. Valley Forge, PA: Judson Press, 1984.

Osbeck, Kenneth W. *The Ministry of Music*. Grand Rapids, MI: Kregel Publications, 1961.

_____. *Singing With Understanding*. Grand Rapids, MI: Kregel Publications, 1979.*

Reynolds, William J. *Survey of Hymnody*. New York, NY: Hold, Rinehart and Winston, Inc., 1963.*

Sallee, James. *A History of Evangelistic Hymnody*. Grand Rapids, MI: Baker Book House, 1978.*

Southern, Eileen. *The Music of Black America: A History*. New York, NY: W. W. Norton and Co., 1983.

Taylor, Jack. *The Hallelujah Factor*. Nashville, TN: Broadman, 1984.

Tozer, A. W. *The Knowledge of the Holy*. New York, NY: Harper and Row, 1978.

_____. *Worship: The Missing Jewel in the Evangelical Church*. Camp Hill, PA: Christian Publications, 1961.

Webber, Robert E. *Worship Is A Verb*. Nashville, TN: Abbott–Martyn, 1992.

_____. ed. *The Topical and Illustrated Library of Christian Worship*. Volumes 1–7. Nashville, TN: Abbott–Martyn, 1992–1994.

_____. *Worship Old & New*. Grand Rapids, MI: Zondervan Publishing House, 1994.

_____. *The Worship Phenomenon*. Nashville, TN: Abbott–Martyn, 1994.

Whaley, Vernon M. *Trends in Gospel Music Publishing: 1940_1960*. Unpublished Ph.D. dissertation. Norman, OK: University of Oklahoma, 1992.

Wiersbe, Warren W. *Real Worship: It Will Change Your Life*. Nashville, TN: Oliver Nelson, 1986.*

Wilhoit, Mel R. "Ira Sankey: Father of Gospel Music" *Rejoice: The Gospel Music Magazine*, June/July 1991.

Wilson, John F. *An Introduction to Church Music*. Chicago, IL: Moody Press, 1965.*

Woods, Ralph L. *The World Treasury of Religious Quotations*. New York, NY: Garland Books, 1966.

* Out of print